More You Know, More You Grow

More You Know, More You Grow

HOW TO GET BETTER EVERY DAY

To Maritza,

I hope this book helps you
get to the top of your mountain.

Grow with Joe

Joe Bautista

Limit Of Liability/Disclaimer Of Warranty

This publication is designed to provide information and motivation to our readers. It is sold with the understanding that the author is not engaged to render any type of psychological, legal, or any other kind of professional advice. The information contained within this publication is strictly for educational purposes. If you wish to apply ideas contained in this publication, you are taking full responsibility for your actions. No warranties or guarantees are expressed or implied by the author's choice to include any of the content in this volume. Neither the publisher nor the individual author(s) shall be liable for any physical, psychological, emotional, financial, or commercial damages, including, but not limited to, special, incidental, consequential or other damages. The fact that an organization or website is referred to in this work as a citation and/or a potential source of further information does not mean that the author or the publisher endorses the information that the organization or Web site may provide or any recommendation it may make.

Acknowledgment

I would like to thank my dad for showing me that hard work can pay off and my mom for showing me how to be a good person. I would also like to thank my wife, Monica, for helping me become a better writer.

Introduction

I believe that you must accumulate skills and knowledge in order to make yourself the best person possible. I see life as a complicated math problem that each person must solve. Initially you don't know how to solve the problem, but you can learn how by discovering what is necessary to solve it. Each person's math problem will be different and will yield a different answer tailored to his or her life.

If you have ever taken calculus, you know that you need different skills to solve each part of the problem. For one area of a problem, you might need algebra, which requires a foundation of addition, subtraction, multiplication, and division. But your math problem is much more complicated than this and will take a lot of time to solve. Things will be much easier once you realize that you need to gain more skills and decide to take the time to learn those skills.

In today's world, it has become easier to learn those skills and gain that knowledge. The internet and books have become the great equalizer. It is so simple to use Google to search a topic or book or to watch an instructional video on YouTube. I remember asking my parents what something meant when I was a kid. Their usual response was, "I don't know. Go look it up in the encyclopedia." And I did. This was a useful skill growing up because I just needed the initiative to look, and I gained the patience to stick with something until I found the answer.

I don't think my parents' generation has that same instinct to immediately turn to the internet. When I ask why they don't look things up on the internet, they explain that they don't think that way. In my eyes, this is fatal. To solve your math problem, you need to seek sources that will help you. I'm not talking about math or grammar skills. I'm talking about acquiring wisdom. Wisdom can come from sources that are free or cost little.

Over the past five years, I have dedicated my life to learning. It started when I read *Random Family* by Adrian LeBlanc — the first non-fiction book I had read in my adult life. I wanted to learn why a Puerto Rican family living in the Bronx continuously made mistakes and how I could avoid the same mistakes. Then my wife, Monica, introduced me to other books, such as *The Tipping Point: How Little Things Can Make a Big Difference* by Malcolm Gladwell. From Gladwell, I learned the power of doing things first — before others did them. When I finished *The Tipping Point*, I found *Outliers: The Story of Success* by Gladwell and *Freakonomics: A Rogue Economist Explores the Hidden Side of Everything* by Stephen J. Dubner and Steven Levitt. Then I became interested in podcasts. With each episode I listened to and every page I read, I learned something new that I could apply to my math problem. I slowly began to solve it and will continue to for the rest of my life.

More You Know, More You Grow is all about being a voracious learner and taking action. I believe I am a much better person for taking this path, and I try to tell others to do the same. Not only does this give you more to talk about, but it can give you new insight on how to solve problems that arise. You will have to experiment to see what works and what doesn't, but continuously learning and taking action will help you become successful down the road. When you have your breakthrough in life, it will all be worth it. To become a diamond, you must endure intense pressure.

I quit watching television so I could dedicate more of my life to this path. When people discuss *Game of Thrones* or *The Walking Dead*, I have no clue what they're talking about. I do follow sports, but I don't watch as many games as I used to. There is too much work to be done to sit on the sidelines and watch time go by. Tai Lopez, one of my favorite influencers, explains that there are three types of people: those who make things happen, those who watch things happen, and those who wonder what happened. Be the person that makes things happen.

Time is the scarcest resource we have because once it's gone, it's gone. Why not maximize life by gaining insight and applying it to become a better person? The first step is realizing that self-improvement is key to achieving happiness in your life. Start out by sitting down and setting up a routine to get things done. I will go over this and other strategies to help you understand what it takes to learn new things and improve your life.

To solve your math problem, you need have a solid foundation of skills, pick up new skills along your journey, and solve your math problem one chunk at a time. This book will talk about the skills I have gained and used on the path to solve my math problem. Although I will never completely solve it, I can get pretty close by constantly growing and persisting. I believe that I will live a better life if, when I die, my math problem is 75 percent complete instead of 10 percent. Sadly, most people tend to only solve a small portion of their math problem.

To solve your math problem you will do a lot of searching, and sometimes you will go down the wrong path, but that's okay. Stories come from the journey, not the destination. There is so much information out there, and thank God for the internet, which allows us to receive a lot of information on the spot. We can buy books at the click of a button, and we immediately receive new recommendations based on a purchase. Podcasts are free to listen to and offer great advice. YouTube videos are also free and can provide information, advice, and motivation in short, concise videos. As you take in this information, see what works for you and disregard the noise.

I want to become an expert in my field — one who sees what is invisible to the amateur. I strongly believe that personal development grows society's pie and offers people greater resources to enjoy. To continue to enlarge this pie, we all must become productive in our respective fields. This is one of my favorite concepts from economics; it puts people in a growth mindset as opposed to a fixed mindset. When we believe that things can get better through practice, skill accumulation, and persistence, those things *will* get better.

Quotes are also very helpful for staying motivated and creating a paradigm shift. A well-stated sentence can move people to do great things. People love it when I tell them one-liners to give them the motivation to act or see things in a new light.

The following are two of my favorite quotes from Les Brown:

"You don't get in life what you want; you get in life what you are."
"Successful people look to the outside to see what they want, and if they can't find it, they go out and create it."

Things rarely come passively, so go out and create the skills necessary to solve your math problem. You have to be active and intentional. Life gets hard, but that's the way life should be. If every day was a good day, you would grow bored and lose motivation.

So far, I have read about 140 books, and my goal is to read 900 more before I pass away. Another goal is to listen to at least 20 hours of podcasts each week. I have learned a lot from what I have already listened to and read, and I am grateful to live in a society where I can take advantage of all these resources. There is no better time to be alive.

I am all about growth because I have seen the results of developing myself and I love to help others grow as well. This is my passion, and I'm so happy that I am able to write this book. (I was able to complete it in 18 months because I stayed with my schedule, doing a little at a time.)

Life is about incremental progress. After reading a handful of books and listening to several podcasts, a light bulb went off in my head. If I become incrementally better each day, in a few years, I will be light years ahead of most people. For the most part, you only see others' highlight reel — the end result of years of hard work. It takes years to become your best, and it is a never-ending journey with many adventures and stories.

This book showcases specific examples of how I use different platforms to make my life better. You can copy exactly what I have done, or you can modify the concepts to fit your liking. Apply this book to your life in whatever way you like, as long as you improve the person you are today. I've been following this routine for about five years, and I keep evolving into a better person.

In certain phases, I have focused my attention on one area of my life that needed improvement. The area on which you focus may be very different than mine, but you will have a better understanding of what you need to do to pursue your goals. I started my learning journey by reading books, then I started listening to podcasts. Soon after, a friend on Facebook posted a motivational speech by Arnold Schwarzenegger, and I was exposed to other motivational speeches thanks to YouTube's algorithms. This is a lifelong process because you will never learn it all, but you can make a pretty good dent and be much better off than if you do nothing.

The basic premise for this book is the belief that you need to improve your life. I did this by investing my time and money in books and classes and actually executing what I learned. I know a lot of people who don't want to do this because they don't want to lose. They would rather obtain a known value from going to a restaurant or a movie than spend time and money on a course. This is because of the psychology concept called "loss aversion." People hate losing twice as much as they enjoy winning. If I found 20 dollars on the side of the road, the impact would be a lot less than if I lost 20 dollars. Life is full of situations and opportunities that might not reach their full potential. Press on. Persevere. Move past lackluster opportunities. Utilize the resources readily available to achieve your best self.

If you need book or podcast recommendations beyond what I cover in this book, please reach out to me at Growwithjoe.me or on Twitter @GrowwithJoe. I look forward to reading your tweets and helping you. Share your reading journey with me on Twitter via #moreyougrow.

Good Artists Copy, Great Artists Steal

I have found that other people provide the best inspiration for determining which path to follow. From podcasts, you can take many ideas and absorb many life lessons. Don't worry about grabbing an idea for yourself. "Good artists copy; great artists steal" is a great saying from Pablo Picasso that can change your life.

I like to take old ideas and make them better; this is what education is all about. It is not about memorizing facts but about understanding that you can use past experiences and lessons to improve your life and make society better. For the majority of my life, I have applied lessons I've learned to different situations to improve them. During my time in the Marine Corps, I learned how to use batch files to perform computer tasks faster, and I applied that knowledge during my internship at the White House. At one point, I had to conduct multiple internet searches for a research topic. Realizing that I would have to do this task over and over during the internship, I remembered that I could accomplish the same task much faster by using a batch file. I saved 30 to 45 minutes per research topic, and at the White House, time is a very scarce resource.

I have incorporated this concept into my life countless times. When I see something I like, I use it to make my life better. This is what education is about — making your life easier by becoming more productive. This will provide you with more income and free time.

This is where books, YouTube videos, and podcasts come in. As I have already discussed, these platforms have great value. However, a majority of that value is left unused. You must dedicate yourself to studying these materials while applying and executing the nuggets of knowledge. Not everything you come across will be easy to do or understand, but repetition will make those things easier.

I dedicate twenty hours per week to podcasts, one hour per day to reading, and one to five hours per week to YouTube videos. Since I drive to work and to meetings, I usually use my BeyondPod Podcast Manger App to listen to the podcast at the top of the queue. Instead of listening to music, you can learn new things to apply to your life. If you like something you hear, write it in a journal or a note-taking app like Evernote.

For reading, I usually dedicate 45 minutes in the morning on the stationary bike at the gym and 15 minutes before bed. I also use the Kindle app on my phone to read a few pages during a down period in my schedule, such as a wait at the doctor's office.

For YouTube videos, I like to watch or simply listen to 15 minutes of motivational speeches — something to give a boost of energy for the day. In everything I do, I look for things that I can apply to my life or to other people's lives. I also appear more knowledgeable when I'm in conversation with others. I appreciate all the work others have done to put topics into digital formats because it has helped me become a better person in this world.

I believe we should strive to live the best lives possible through incremental increases in skills and knowledge. By continuously acquiring lessons and wisdom, you will grow one percent every day. One of the best lessons I have learned is from a quote by Jim Rohn: "You are the average of the five people you spend the most time with." You must decide what type of person you want to become. If you constantly watch non-informative media or play games on your phone, you will become that average. I try to limit excess garbage in my life because I don't feel that it makes me one percent better as a person.

Finding new people to help you improve can be difficult and requires time and effort. A great way to accomplish this is to join a Meetup group or a professional association. You can attend events without your friends and meet other like-minded individuals.

If you're socially awkward, like I was for most of my life, I suggest you follow *The Art of Charm* podcast by Jordan Harbinger. Each week, he hosts a guest to help his listeners become better people, and the website offers a toolbox that will increase your social intelligence. This is my favorite podcast because of its many valuable tools.

The Art of Charm offers many great tips to help you socially engineer your life, and it suggests books and other podcasts. I highly recommend that you go to *The Art of Charm* website and click on the "best of podcast" link. *The Art of Charm* was so inspiring to me that it finally convinced me to go to the boot camp Harbinger always talks about. I wish I had found this podcast earlier in my life, but as Robert Greene says, there are no good or bad events; there are just events. Ruminating will not help. I just need to look forward and consider how to achieve my next goal.

Tai Lopez's podcast is my second favorite because he is a renaissance man. He reads a great deal and shares what he learns from his mentors. I've been listening to his stuff since 2014, and he is good. Some people don't like him because he likes to jump around from topic to topic, but I have gleaned a lot of good information from him. He motivated me to read 36 books each year, the average number that CEOs read annually. He offers a lot of good advice and he ultimately hopes to bring more professionals to his programs to help entrepreneurs. In addition to his podcast, he is very active on Snapchat.

Lopez says that many people are boring because they don't have anything interesting to say in a conversation. This is one reason I like to listen to his podcast — I receive helpful tips about what to say in conversations, particularly with new people I meet. I was amazed to hear that 60 percent of college graduates never read another book. (This fact is probably a major reason that television rules what happens around us.) Lopez encourages learning and using lessons taught in books to give ourselves "the good life," as he calls it.

Podcasts are great for when you're commuting to work, running errands, or working out. There are no truly original ideas because people just take ideas from multiple sources and combine them into something new. This is called innovation. The majority of what we do is based on using our past experiences and knowledge to improve what has already been done.

It is not enough to make something you're working on two times better; you must make it at least ten times better to make the change you want in life. To understand the importance of this concept, read *Zero to One* by Peter Thiel. Using the examples of Tesla and Google, Thiel demonstrates how innovation should take place. Tesla was a car ten times better than other electric cars, and Google was ten times better than other search engines when people started to switch over. I try to figure out ways to personally become ten times better through podcasts, YouTube videos, and books. I usually have to practice my craft over and over again, utilizing new strategies I stole, but in most cases, I do become ten times better.

New knowledge can also make me seem more interesting. For example, I'm good at giving business tips because I follow James Altucher and Gary Vanyerchuk. I advised my sister, who styles hair, to expand her business by collaborating with someone with a lot of followers. This will give her access to a larger crowd and help her show off her skills. I learned this trick from James Altucher, who said you shouldn't focus too much energy on your own blog; find someone with a huge crowd, post content to their site, and direct traffic back to you through a link. They have the followers and people are always looking for good content because it saves them time. It's a win-win situation. I wouldn't know this tip if I didn't spend time learning from wise people.

I regularly listen to *The Art of Charm*, *Achieve Your Goals*, *The James Altucher Show*, *The Tai Lopez "Book Of The Day" Show*, *$100 MBA*, and *The Tim Ferriss Show*. These podcasts have tremendous value, and my life has greatly improved since I discovered them. The hosts feature amazing guests and dig into what made them successful. From these podcasts, I receive new tips on how to live my life to the fullest. I try to use those tips in my life and see if they work for me. (Remember to write down the tips because you will not remember what you hear.)

I used to listen to *Stuff You Should Know* and *This American Life*, but I feel like my time has shrunk and I can't listen to all the podcasts I followed before I became a financial advisor. I gave those podcasts up because they were not helping me grow as a person as much as other podcasts. Sometimes you need to cut things out of your life to accomplish your goals. This is one reason I sold my television. I rarely used it, it was just collecting dust in my living room. I decided to sell it and dedicate more of my time to obtaining knowledge to become more innovative.

No matter what topic you're interested in, there is a podcast for you. I used to think that I had to listen to everything, but the BeyondPod Podcast Manager app allows me to skip 30 seconds ahead, and I can skip stories and ads that I don't think are interesting or useful. I learned this tip from *Extreme Productivity* by Robert Pozen. In this book, Pozen explains that he reads various newspapers every day but is selective in what he reads from each source. For example, he reads the Financial Times only for international news and the Wall Street Journal only for local news. You have to know what you want and then be selfish with your time because you can't create another hour.

Another great tip is to listen to podcasts on double speed. This will sound weird at first — like a heavy metal sound — but you will get used to it after about an hour. This will cut your time spent in half. You will breeze through podcasts and make more progress with your life. Gulp life; don't sip it. Try to absorb as many materials as you can, but don't drown yourself. Slowly build yourself up. It will be uncomfortable, but it will get easier with time. You just have to perform each activity continuously.

By taking in all this new knowledge, you will be able to pick out which items are the best for you and apply them to your life. This is the main reason I started a book club. I wanted people to read books, pick out the best lessons, and determine how to apply the lessons to their life. I'm constantly trying to make my life better, and I do this through new ideas. I don't know all the answers or where I am going all the time, but I know I can get the answers from asking questions, reading books, listening to podcasts, and watching videos. You can make things better, but you must expend effort. I love that I have access to so many podcasts, books, and YouTube videos because I have an edge over previous generations.

In the video *The 50th Law Chapter 3*, Robert Greene explains that there are no good or bad events; there are just events. I found this eye-opening because past events have made you the person that you are now because of the actions you took. Greene explains that a perceived bad event, such as losing your job, could have actually been a good thing because it finally pushed you to do the activity you always wanted to do. In contrast, a perceived good event, such as winning the lottery, could be a bad thing; most lottery winners go bankrupt because they are not used to the new lifestyle and the attention it brings.

To reach more events, you must be active. This will cause you to have interactions with other people and things. In the book *The Black Swan: The Impact of the Highly Improbable*, Nassim Taleb explains that highly improbable events can change your life. To experience these positive highly improbable events, you must be available. Exposure is key, and meeting new people will get you there. This is why he says it is important to attend happy hours with other people because you never know who you will come across. If you just go home and watch television, you're not setting yourself up for success. The likelihood of gaining a fantastic opportunity while sitting at home is not very high, that's why I decided to sell my television. It's okay not to go to a happy hour or some type of meetup every night, but you need to establish a process for meeting other people.

As Russ Roberts discusses in his book *How Adam Smith Can Change Your Life*, self-sufficiency is the road to poverty. Go out and see how you can help people and provide opportunities for them while seeing what opportunities come your way. It will never be a one-to- one exchange, but you can make the world a better place by offering value for others to collect.

Don't become discouraged about losing a few hours. Maintain an explorer mindset that allows you to attain a goal after putting in a lot of effort. Loss aversion and the idea of failure slow down many people, but persistence and dedication are the keys to the majority of success. Just stick with something, and eventually you will become so good that no one will be able to ignore you.

The main takeaway from other people's success stories is simply hard, hard work. Even if you fail or lose a lot of money, you must learn to pick yourself up and repeat or make a change in your process to become more productive. You may spend 20 dollars on a book that you know isn't for you after you read only a few pages. The best thing to do is simply quit reading and find something else to do or skip sections that you know will not benefit you. You don't have to read the whole book just because you bought it. *Freakonomics*, a podcast with a lot of good advice, taught me this lesson. One of my favorite episodes involves the concept of the sunk-cost fallacy, which states that you won't recoup your funds from a failed activity, no matter how much more money and effort you expend. It is better just to give up and try something different. This is especially true with movies or television shows. If a movie is awful after the first 15 to 30 minutes, you should choose a different movie or just do something else. I had to let go of a few podcasts because they stopped teaching me anything. At first they were great, but eventually they became stale for me. I usually find new podcasts through guests that appear on podcasts I have listened to. I have stopped following many podcasts, but the new value and time gained from not listening to them is making me a much better person overall. Learning to let go is hard, but it is necessary for success.

I've read a lot of books and listened to a lot of podcasts and many of them have similar themes and messages. In this book you will be exposed to some recurring themes and messages but hopefully you're able to see them more clearly. To have a message come through and use it, you have to be exposed to it many times or hear it at a certain point in your life when it is salient. This book doesn't have to be read in order and I suggest that you flip through the sections that you don't like and only read the ones that peak your interest. Use what you can and just forget the rest.

If You're Not Growing, You're Dying

Life is all about change. Things will never stay the same, and if you choose to continuously live the same life, you will be left behind to struggle. A great book that talks about the need for change is *Who Moved My Cheese* by Spencer Johnson. It can be read in one to two hours, and it helps the reader to view difficult situations as transition points not end points.

When faced with a difficult situation, most people let their emotions hinder them from obtaining their goals. This causes them to fail in life. The discerning person will understand that life is not fair and that things can change. That person will become successful by realizing that things will deteriorate if he or she doesn't go out alone and make some changes.

I firmly believe that if you're failing to take action, you're failing in life. Life is all about execution. A lot of people want to talk about becoming better, but far too many people are waiting on the sidelines. In *Who Moved My Cheese*, Johnson explains that it might be difficult and scary to go find your "cheese," but the goal of a successful life requires you to do so. The first couple of steps are always the hardest, but it tends to become easier as we keep going. Don't be like the characters Hem and Haw in *Who Moved My Cheese*, who waited for success to come to them. As Marva Collins said, "Success doesn't come to you — you go to it."

I strongly believe that doing something at 40 to 80 percent efficiency is much better than doing nothing at all. At least we're learning and building habits for change. The world is constantly changing around us, and we must learn to grow as people because "the cheese" will move and we must find it.

I love change because I constantly want to get better. Other people might complain about getting older, but I enjoy it because I see myself as a better person than I was six months ago and I will be an even better person six month from now. I don't need to do the same things I did in my early twenties. I'm really enjoying life, and I can see things getting better.

Everything I do is about expanding opportunities and pushing myself to greatness. I hate using the word "good" because I want to be great and eventually relentless, as Tim Grover (Michael Jordan and Kobe Bryant's personal trainer) says. Self-improvement is the way to be great. As an economist, I know I can't be the best at everything, and that's why I need to focus on the one or two areas in which I want to be great. This is known as "division of labor." If I focus on what I'm great at and other people focus on what they're great at, we can create a society that is happier and more productive.

Don't be a generalist that wonders; be a specialist that gets things done. Far too many people spread themselves thin and live in mediocrity. Another key thing is balance between the social, professional, and physical aspects of your life. You can make everything happen, but maybe not all at once. To improve these various parts of your life, you must be intentional. It is not enough to want improvement. You must work and plan.

When it comes to planning out your life, you should spend three percent of your income on knowledge or gaining new skills. If you're not growing, you're dying. Far too many people don't take the time to improve themselves spiritually, mentally, and physically, and it shows in their lifestyles. I recommend that you spend your money on a skill that will improve your life because success comes when preparation meets opportunity. If you're not prepared for the opportunity, it will be picked up by someone else.

There are really no shortcuts in life. It takes time and deliberate practice to make everything come together. In an excellent book called *Bounce: The Myth of Talent and the Power of Practice*, Matthew Syed explains Anders Ericsson's research that about 10,000 hours of deliberate practice are required for an individual to become an expert at any topic. This practice must receive feedback and must address some of your deficiencies. When you take it easy, you won't get better. You must get used to failure and seek a mentor to help you along the way. Michael Jordan had Phil Jackson and Tim Grover. If your team is strong, you will be stronger as a person. You might have to cut negative people out of your life, but it will be for your own benefit.

I strongly believe that you must work harder on yourself than you do on anything else. Doing this will help you handle "life." And you need to be prepared for life because life will never make an appointment with you. When life happens, it will set you back in terms of money, time, and your health. When you focus on growing yourself, you're making your inner circle stronger to handle life and give you more opportunities to succeed. Your inner circle consists of mental, spiritual, and physical elements. As the great John Wooden said, "You will never outperform your inner circle." So make sure that every day, even if just for 10 minutes, you put energy into growing your inner circle. In addition to books, podcasts, and YouTube videos, I've also learned invaluable lessons from friends, family, and life in general. All of these things and people have helped to grow my inner circle. I've made my life a lot easier by internalizing the lessons in this book, and I can't wait to see how these lessons will help you too.

How Quitting My Job Changed My Life

In the life-changing podcast episode "The Upside of Quitting" by *Freakonomics*, host Stephen Dubner talks about the sunk-cost fallacy and why you should quit certain things. When I first moved to D.C., I was a valet driver for a few months, and I often thought, "Man, I have to do more with my life." This was at the height of the financial recession, and finding a job was difficult, so I had to take what I could get. When I landed a position with the federal government, I thought I freaking made it. I had job security and a position I thought was a good fit.

I was able to find a job in the federal government because of my veteran status as a United States Marine. Like many people I wanted a job in the federal government because of the stability offered. I began my federal career as an administrative assistant. I saw this as a stepping stone to another position within the federal government. However, I soon realized that this was not the career for me because it was just like the Marine Corps — a fixed mindset where things were held together by bureaucracy and politics. I especially grew upset when the Secretary of Defense said that there would be mandatory furloughs to deal with budget cuts. I was working in a career that I didn't like and was told what I could and couldn't have. My cheese was starting to stink, and I knew I could do better.

A few months into my job at the Pentagon, I hated life. I didn't want to be there, and this affected my relationship with my wife because I was constantly in a bad mood or complaining. The job environment was bad for me, and I sometimes took sick days because I couldn't stand going to work. I really needed those mental health days. I lost my passion because the job didn't fit my strengths and the bureaucracy was killing me. I felt that I was just treading water and that I had to wait for people to retire to receive a promotion. It was a fixed-mindset career without the possibility of change. My strengths require a less bureaucratic structure and I do best in an environment that provides autonomy, creativity, and control. "The Upside of Quitting" episode changed my life, and I realized that I needed to quickly make a change. A few co-workers urged me to leave because I had too much potential - I made my escape plan soon afterward. Because of my GI Bill benefits, I decided to go back to school to study economics.

Quitting my secure job was the best decision I've made. Instead of talking about leaving or just waiting for that federal government retirement, I took action, quit, and made my life better. By taking an interest in learning new things, I was able to see why it was best to quit my job and try to start my own business. I gain a lot of wisdom through the podcasts that I listen to, and this is the main reason I eat up so much knowledge. If I hadn't heard those words on the *Freakonomics* podcast, I would probably still be at my federal job, hating life. Immediately quitting your job might not be the best step for you. Sometimes you need a strategy and a plan. At other times, you just need to *do*.

When I left my job at the Pentagon, I tried to create a business that combined financial planning with personal training. While I was working on my business and going to school, I listened to entrepreneurship podcasts like *Starting from Nothing*, *INspired INsiders*, and *Entrepreneur on Fire*. I tried to accumulate as much information as possible to make myself successful. I even joined an entrepreneurship group in D.C. through Meetup and attended events. I learned a lot about what it would take to start a business and how to move forward, but I also realized that I didn't want to train people every day as a personal trainer. Too much effort was required to create a business that focused on individual personal training and financial planning, and financial planning won. Eventually, I realized that I solely wanted to stick with financial planning because of its flexibility and the fact that I personally desired financial freedom.

Quitting can be one of the best things. You have to know when to fold the cards. Don't let your ego get in the way of a pragmatic decision, and don't look at something that doesn't work out as a failure. Although I quit my job as a personal trainer to focus on financial planning, I learned a lot from being a personal trainer and gained skills that will help me in the future. It was an opportunity to learn that personal training was not the path for me, and I now have a better understanding of what I want out of life.

If you are not happy with something and feel like you should quit, listen to the "The Upside of Quitting." It changed my life for the better and now I'm doing something I want to do.

I quit my job and went back to school. I am grateful that a fellow federal employee told me I should leave. He knew I had more potential than what the position and the federal government could offer. I'm a worker and creator, and I love to keep busy. This is why I love my job as a business owner and financial advisor. I am responsible for my success and for the success of my clients. I keep moving forward, and self-improvement is key to helping me get where I want to be. I love that I am able to live in the United States and make myself better on a daily basis. My cheese is always going to move, and I need to keep up with that change by dedicating time to learn and grow.

Life is all about options. The more options you have, the better off you tend to be because you won't end up stuck with what you don't like. However, options come from having resources, and trading one resource for another takes time and requires the building of relationships. Tai Lopez wonderfully explains that instead of making a pros and cons list, you should make an options list. One pro can be more valuable than ten cons if things go your way.

When you stick with your old cheese, you risk missing opportunities. If you hold on too long, the cheese might get moldy. There is risk in everything we do, and one of the primary rules of accepting risk is to be compensated for that risk if things work out.

Being an entrepreneur pushed me into self-improvement, and I love it because I'm achieving new levels of success. Over the past two years, I have been upping my game as I try to improve myself, and I've seen tremendous gains in my personal and business life. I've always been highly motivated to reach my goals, but I haven't always worked in the most effective ways. Thanks to the internet, I've been able to find different things that pique my interest, and I'm always looking for new material to make me a better person. I want to make a difference in this world, and being the best possible "me" will make the biggest impact.

Why You Should Invest in Yourself

I often find that people don't have goals or plans to back up their goals. I like to tell people that a goal without a plan is just a dream. Figuring out what you want in life is crucial. You need a sense of direction — a sense of where you want to go. You might not know all the time, but knowing 80–90 percent of the time is pretty good. It took me my entire 20s to actually figure out what I wanted to do in life, but because I invested in myself, I had a pretty good idea of which direction I needed to go.

Again, I recommend that you follow Les Brown's advice about shutting off your television and turning on your life. Watching a lot of television replaces educational opportunities that could have a positive impact on your earning potential. There are far too many opportunities in this world, and you don't want to lose them. Opportunities aren't missed. They're simply picked up by other people.

Instead of watching television, read more. In the book *The Miracle Morning*, Hal Elrod talks about the need for reading. I'm a huge believer in the concept that readers are leaders. I try to read at least three books a month. (I keep track of them through Goodreads.com, and I typically buy them through Amazon because I love that Amazon gives book recommendations.) I spend less time reading fiction books; I probably read two to four each year. Fiction books provide some great lessons, but I gain more satisfaction and knowledge from reading non-fiction.

I go through phases in terms of what type of books I read. A few years ago, I read about nine books on behavioral economics, and I was able to use the concepts I learned in my day-to-day job as a financial advisor. Later, as I was trying to grow my business I focused on books that helped me do that. Right now, I'm reading autobiographies of famous people in sports because I enjoy reading about the grind that got them to the top. A Google search on what type of book you should read will give you a great start. If you read 20–30 pages each day, you can basically read two books each month. This will provide you with new skills and insights on how to take on the world.

One book that has really influenced me is *The Millionaire Next Door* by Thomas Stanley. While the ending was subpar, the first 90 percent was on point. Stanley provides a clear understanding of what it takes to "make it." He explains that the basic key to achieving financial success is living on less than you earn — paying yourself first and avoiding debt. I strongly believe in this, but situations might arise in your life in which you will need to take on some debt to achieve your goals. You can do two things with your time and money: consume them or invest them. Investing them will lead to growth and higher levels of productivity. If you consume too much of your time and money, you will remain static and won't be able to keep up with the changing environment.

From ages 13 to 31, Bill Gates spent his life learning how to write computer code. A young Warren Buffett spent his time reading all the books on investing in his local library. These people took the time to invest in their craft to move from amateurs to professionals. If you want to make a difference, you have to become a master at your profession. People seek out masters because they want the comfort of knowing that someone with experience is providing them wisdom and guidance.

To get this experience, you need to learn from others through face-to-face discussions, videos, podcasts, and books. Many of the difficult and confusing things we come across have already been experienced by others. Fortunately, many of these people thought it beneficial to record and share their thoughts.

The biggest benefit I receive from focusing on reading and learning is that I can share my knowledge with other people and use it in my day-to-day life. Over the past few years, I have been able to use one-liners I've learned to help my clients pursue their goals and take action. People appreciate this. Lately I've been telling people to write option lists instead of pros and cons lists because decisions need to be based on value, not what's good or bad. People are impressed by this, I receive credit for helping them out, and they're better off for hearing the information.

I love to take old things and make them better. I take ideas from economics, psychology, and business to create something new, yet familiar. I'm able to do this because I put in the effort to learn new things and experience the unknown.

In today's world, you can become a specialist and do pretty well. I might not know how to fix a car or perform open heart surgery, but I'm a master when it comes to financial planning because I studied economics, took a certified financial planning prep course, and am working as a financial advisor. According to a Hewitt Study, four out of five Americans are not expected to meet all of their financial needs in retirement, and there is a need for a great financial advisor to educate these people. One of my passions is to help more people make it to retirement so the "four out of five" number is reduced.

The journey will not be easy, but you must desire success badly. This is the theme of many motivational videos. In Eric Thomas's YouTube video *How Bad Do You*, he talks about the secrets to success. It is very motivating, and his story about the student and teacher is eye-opening. I cannot do the video justice by retelling it, so I strongly recommend that you watch it for yourself. Eric speaks with a lot of passion, and this works for me, but it might not be for everyone.

One of the best investments you can make is investing in yourself. I find it very fulfilling to learn and use the knowledge I accumulated because it helps me operate at a higher level. If you don't let life distract you from investing in yourself, you'll be fine in the long term. I only have so much time left on this planet, and I want to make sure I'm executing at my best.

Throughout this book, I will mention many other books that are highly influential. However, don't spend all of your time reading. You have to actually go out in the world and do something with the knowledge and wisdom you receive. Execution is key to obtaining a great life. In *The Grand Theory of Everything* podcast, Tai Lopez talks about the importance of K.S.E. (knowledge, strategy, and execution). Execution is important because most people never take the shot to become great. As Wayne Gretzky used to say, "You miss 100 percent of the shots you don't take."

A key to success is trying without fear of failing. *Arnold's 6 Rules of Success* is a great YouTube video on the topic. Arnold Schwarzenegger lays out his rules for success, and he explains that executing is a big part of his success. If you want the full story, watch his 2009 University of Southern California commencement speech, which breaks down the process even more. I even took a screenshot of the frame that shows the six rules and set it as my computer wallpaper. My favorite line is "You can't climb the ladder of success with your hands in your pockets." This is so true because only hard, hard work will help you achieve your goals.

Here are the six rules:

- Trust yourself
- Break the rules
- Don't be afraid of failing
- Don't listen to the naysayers
- Work like hell (the most important one)
- Give something back

Know Where to Focus Your Energy

One of Tai Lopez's most realistic insights is that time and decay move in the same direction. Think about it: If you never make an effort to maintain your house, in 30 years no one will want to live there. But if you put energy into the upkeep of that house, people will buy it for more than you paid for it. You must make the effort to become great to avoid decay.

One of my biggest life passions is to become the best person I can become. If I'm the best version of myself, I'm going to live a better life. I don't want to wake up one day and say, "What happened?" I believe this tends to happen when we let life dictate where we go. It takes a lot of work to resist what life hands out. Many temptations try to hinder us, and it's easy to get caught up in the distractions that life has to offer. When you don't put energy into growing yourself, you let decay creep in.

One of the best books on this topic is *Good to Great* by Jim Collins. The principles in this book will help you understand how you need to focus your energy. For instance, Collins explains that you must focus your energy on being a workhorse instead of a show horse and that you must be sure to have self-motivated people on your bus so you're not wasting your energy on telling people what to do or keeping them accountable to the overall mission. I also love his hedgehog concept: You should do something you can be great at, can make money from, and have a passion for. If you spend your time on other things outside of this concept, then you're not fully maximizing your potential in life.

To be successful in your career, figure out what your strengths are, what you are really passionate about, and what makes you money. This is the premise of the "hedgehog concept" in *Good to Great* by Jim Collins. As Collins explains, successful companies such as Gillette have used this concept to become great. Most people think the enemy of "great" is "bad." However, according to Collins, the real enemy is "good" because if you're satisfied with good, you'll never be great. Always aiming for greatness takes more effort, but it will be worth it when you reach your goals.

For now, my definition of greatness is taking advantage of opportunities that push my boundaries to new levels of success. I am hardwired to work hard and make a positive impact in my environment, and these concepts help me progress toward my definition of greatness. I attribute this to my dad. When I was a child, my dad worked every damn day to provide for his family. On some days, after he finished his regular job, he did side projects to earn even more. He dug and moved trees at a plant nursery, doing back-breaking work to make his family's dream come true.

My dad is an immigrant from Oaxaca, Mexico, and he crossed the border to the United States because of the opportunities offered. He wanted to be here so badly that he was sent back to Mexico five times and came back six. He refused to settle for the status quo. I saw this as a child, and I now want to be successful and take advantage of all the opportunities I can. If I don't, I believe I will be doing myself and my dad a disservice.

My parents didn't save for my college, but that was because it was hard for them to do something they didn't know how to do. However, I knew I needed an education to have access to higher-paying careers. I applied to Gonzaga University and the University of Oregon and was accepted at both, but as soon as I saw the price tag, I decided the military was the best route for me. I was fortunate to not have to find a way to pay back student loans because I would have graduated in 2008, during the Great Recession. One of my strengths is that I like to plan stuff out and see the best options. Joining the Marine Corps provided me with a way to pay for college but also many life lessons and an appreciation for what life offers. Even though I had some of my worst days in the Marine Corps, I would definitely go back and do it all over again because it made me the strong person I am today.

I originally wanted to join the Air Force, but the Air Force recruiter didn't have time to see me when I called the office. My two closest friends in high school had already signed up with the Marine Corps recruiter, and they convinced me to see him, too. By describing the greatness of the Marine Corps and how it would help me become a better person, and by explaining that one-third of Fortune 500 CEOs were Marines, the recruiter convinced me. (I no longer think the part about the CEOs is true, but the story did convince me to join the best military branch.) The recruiter even made me stand on my chair and yell "I want to become a Marine!" I had always wanted to achieve more in life, and the Marine Corps helped me become a better person through its vigorous training program and disciplined structure. To improve our strengths, we must do things outside of our comfort zones.

When I left active duty, mediocrity was not the life for me. This is one reason I couldn't stand my jobs before I became a financial advisor. If I work 70 hours a week, I want to make sure I'm compensated more than the person who only puts 50 percent effort into his 40-hour week. When, as a federal employee, I took a look around, I felt this was happening to some of my colleagues. This is why I love my current job as a financial advisor. I'm doing something that I'm great at, that gives me purpose, and that I can use to make the change I want to see in the world. Focusing on my strengths in an area that makes me happy fuels me and allows me to work even harder.

I encourage you to take personality tests to help you decide what areas are ideal for you to put your energy into and what type of people you work well with. I have found that personality tests are very helpful. When I took the DiSC assessment, I found that I am a conscientious person and an analyst. It is crazy how accurate these tests can be, and taking one can help you understand how you operate as a person and which options you should choose in life.

Understanding the person that you are is something that will help you make money and help you live the best version of your life. Some of the biggest mistakes people make are operating in a field in which little money can be made or taking on too much debt to pursue their goals. For a while, I thought about being a personal trainer full-time. I did personal training while I was going to school, but it didn't bring in very much money, and I was not passionate about making it a full-time gig after I graduated. Personal training is now a hobby for me because I'm not interested in making it a career.

Having passion about your field can help you stay disciplined. Disciplined thoughts and disciplined actions are keys to success. It is also important to create a "stop list" to keep you disciplined and focused on your goals, which I learned from one of my mentors, Philip Leopold. If you can't be great at something or it's not helping you become great, either stop doing it or delegate the task to someone else. You only have 24 hours in a day, and you have to use those 24 hours effectively by putting your energy into the right things and staying disciplined by focusing on actions that will help you pursue your goals. This might not be possible initially, but you should develop a plan to stop doing things that do not progress your life and waste your energy.

Another concept that I like in *Good to Great* is that you should create "big hairy audacious goals." As Les Brown says, failure is usually a result of setting goals that are too reachable. Goals should be uncomfortable, requiring you to stretch yourself to do something new. If you want to become a better runner, you need to do an exercise routine that will make you feel uncomfortable — one that involves sweating, hard breathing, and exhaustion. Then, when you do the exercise at the same pace the following week, your body will have adapted and you can perform a little better. This is an effective use of your energy for the day.

Being uncomfortable is where greatness is made. People who don't push themselves waste opportunities. Billions of people don't have the opportunities that I do; am I going to waste them? I don't think so. I only have a finite amount of energy, so I'm going to focus on things that will provide more opportunities and value to those around me.

My two biggest passions are health and personal finance. I am passionate about health because during my youth I was obese. I never want to return to my unhealthy childhood habits. To stay healthy, I put energy into going to the gym, which helps me stay mentally and physically strong each day. When I go to the gym, I don't have to think twice about what I need to do, and I don't waste energy because, from my time as a personal trainer, I have the knowledge and experience to do a proper workout. From my public health degree, I know the value of being healthy and that health can disappear if you don't put energy into it. If you don't know how to exercise or eat healthy, ask someone for help or seek the information on your own. Either way, you have to take some type of action.

When I got out of the Marine Corps in 2011, I went directly to school. I originally wanted to become a physical therapist, but the job bored me, so I decided to go into healthcare management. I chose public health for my initial undergrad degree, but things changed when I took my first economics class. After finishing my second degree in economics, I was soon on track for financial advising because I had always been passionate about personal finance due to my humble upbringing.

One classic topic you study in economics is comparative advantage[1]. Having a comparative advantage means that you have strengths in one area over another and you can produce things at a higher rate by focusing on that one area. As much as possible, it's better to focus on your strengths and delegate your weaker activities to others. I'm good at reading books and remembering useful tips and facts, so this is my strength and the reason I'm writing this book. Even though I like to write, I am not very good at grammar and sentence structure. This is why I hired an edi-

---

1 Comparative Advantage: the ability of an individual or group to carry out a particular economic activity (such as making a specific product) more efficiently than another activity.

Absolute Advantage: the ability of an individual or group to carry out a particular economic activity more efficiently than another individual or group.

tor. When people focus on their strengths, society's pie grows because society is more productive and has more to trade. If you're weak in a certain area, you can focus on making it a strength, but you have to make sure it's worth it to you in the long run. I'm not the best writer now, but I'm willing to focus my time on writing because I like it and I know it will provide me new opportunities in the future.

We don't live in a zero-sum world. We must strive to enlarge the pie, and that happens when a population takes the time to focus on its strengths and improves itself. I will make a difference in my lifestyle and for society, but it will come with time, determination, and persistence. I will get tired and face obstacles, but my determination will push me through because I refuse to be good when I can be great. My parents sacrificed too much for me to be anything less than great, and I want to maximize my life.

I grew up in a mobile home as the child of two blue-collar workers, but attending economically diverse schools showed me that there were career opportunities different from what my parents did. I always enjoyed reading my savings account statement to see how much interest I accrued. When I took a class in personal finance in high school, I was especially interested in learning how to grow my money, and I wanted to offer advice for others to do the same.

In terms of a career, personal finance won out because it was the easier of the two to implement, but I still use my public health degree to make myself a better financial advisor. Without my study of public health, I wouldn't have been led to behavioral economics. Behavioral economics is about using people's behaviors to help them make better decisions. I found this fascinating. I read nine books on the subject, and now I often use the concepts to help others.

The first book you should read about behavior and habits is *The Power of Habit* by Charles Duhigg, which talks about the cue, routine, and reward cycle that causes people to do certain habits. Understanding how your habits work in that cycle and having control over them will help you pursue your goals. As the saying goes, "If you knew better, you would do better." You can control yourself for the most part, but you have to study yourself and your environment.

If you want to get deeper into psychology, I recommend *Thinking, Fast and Slow* by Daniel Kahneman. This very thick book is based strongly on theory. It doesn't contain fun stories such as those in *The Power of Habit*, but it presents a lot of powerful material. As Kahneman explains, overall, if you want to become an expert in a particular subject matter, you need to put in the time by focusing your studies on books, podcasts, and practical applications in that field. One rule of thumb to becoming an expert is to read nine books in that area. Doing this should bring you pretty close to being a go-to person in that field.

I didn't have every opportunity growing up, but I'm making the best of it now that I'm older and have more options. I gained these options by putting energy into pursuing knowledge and taking advantage of opportunities to gain new experiences. I joined the military, studied abroad, interned at the White House, and met different people around the world, and I have grown a lot as a person from these experiences. I love putting energy into growing myself because I am a much better person now than I ever was in the past.

How I Keep It Moving

To maintain the will to go forward, I drink hard from the motivational speeches and stories Kool-Aid. While I get ready for the day, I watch motivational videos and listen to motivational podcasts and songs like "Started From the Bottom" by Drake, and write in my journal three things that I am grateful for and one small victory. (In addition, I try to hang around positive people; negative people zap motivation.) One of my favorite quotes from Zig Ziglar is "Motivation is like bathing — it is recommended daily."

If you search "motivational videos" on YouTube, you'll find thousands and thousands of videos. I recommend creating a YouTube playlist out of your favorite videos. Check out Les Brown, Eric Thomas, Mel Robbins, and Zig Ziglar. YouTube is great at giving recommendations, and when you find one that lifts your spirits, click the "add" button. I haven't found many motivational videos that prominently feature women, but if you come across a really good one, please tweet me @GrowWithJoe. When I'm feeling down, I usually resort to videos to get me through my day. I especially like to listen to them while I get ready in the morning. Motivational podcasts like *The Art of Charm* are also great in the morning. Find what works best for you.

Motivation and discipline are the keys to help you move forward with life. Some days I don't want to do anything. The process of accomplishing a certain goal can be boring or overwhelming. A key to continued growth is motivated action — finding a reason to keep moving forward. *Are You Hungry* by Les Brown is the first place I go when I feel unmotivated; it helps put me in the right mindset. After listening to Les Brown, I try to focus my attention on the next step I need to take instead of worrying about completing the whole process.

If you want to accomplish great things, having the motivation to keep going will help. When I was in the Marines, motivation was huge. There is a reason so many running cadences are about motivation. The thing with motivation is that you have to accept it. I'm not a rah-rah type person, but I feel better when I watch the videos, and afterward, I immediately do something in pursuit of my goals.

You won't be motivated every day, and I don't think you can be. When I'm unmotivated, I usually find that I'm overwhelmed and need to recharge my batteries. To revamp, I like to do yoga or go for walks, and I have found that sitting in a sauna helps clear my mind. When I do these things, I feel much better and ready to take on my day. Breaks are very valuable — they can help reset your mind and make you friendlier when you're dealing with people.

Another key for motivation is knowing your "why." If you wander around without working on your purpose, motivational videos won't help. For me, they set the tone for the day. I have my goals, and I know the steps I need to take to progress. Use the tools around you. Find what works, whether it be a vision board, an accountability partner, or motivational speeches. Just keep moving forward on your journey toward bettering yourself.

Going by Mindsight, Not by Eyesight

It's amazing that people can work hard for many years without any reward. They press on because they choose to go by mindsight and not eyesight, as Les Brown says in his video *Mindsight over Eyesight*.

When people work by mindsight, they operate on the "why," and they have the habits in place to make themselves work hard. In the book *Start with Why*, Simon Sinek describes the process perfectly by introducing the Golden Circle. If you start by thinking why you're doing something instead of what you're doing, you'll be much more effective in sticking with it and demonstrating value. This will be the fuel that gets your vehicle going. It will also bring a much more personal touch to your life.

Understanding your "why" will greatly increase your odds of working hard. Even if you're not doing what you want to do right now, understanding the "why" will help you stay motivated and help you keep grinding and hustling toward your dreams. The dreams are free, but the hustle is sold separately. Steve Harvey does an excellent job explaining this in the video *The Dream is Free*.

Sinek says that most people quit because they focus on the "what" and "how" instead of the "why." People who start a new career by thinking about "what" they plan to do are more likely to fail. Similarly, when I worked as a personal trainer, I noticed that those who didn't stick with their routines didn't properly understand their "why" for working out.

Reading *Start with Why* gave me insight on how I should operate. I must start with "why," move to "how," and end with "what."

Now that I have this mindsight in place, I hope to be a much more effective financial advisor. I grew up with my parents and sisters in a mobile home, and no one was available to give them the technical financial advice and inspiration to become the best financial version of themselves. I also discovered that no such person lived in my community during my time in the Marines and my first few years in D.C. I remember that, while I was growing up, family members didn't have a coach or mentor around to help them make the right financial decisions. We squandered windfalls and made financial mistakes. This is my "why." I want to help people have financial abundance to reduce their stress and prevent them from struggling.

I keep hearing that Latinos have a low net worth, and that really bugs me. A 2015 article in *The Atlantic* titled, "Why So Many Minority Millennials Can't Get Ahead", claimed that minorities have a lower net worth than whites. The very first story described how the author was trying to save for a down payment for a home but received a phone call from her mother, who needed assistance in paying for the funeral of her dad. So the author relabeled her house fund as the funeral fund. It's these kind of stories that I would like to prevent from becoming reality for Latinos. Recently one of my wife's uncles passed away, and it was up to her and some family members to pick up the pieces because he didn't have the resources to pay for the funeral. This created some financial stress, and I was immediately reminded of the article in *The Atlantic*.

Stories like these are my "why" to work hard. There was a time when all I wanted to do was work 40 hours per week and get out of my office job. Now I'm in a career with a clearly defined "why," and I could work 60–80 hours per week with a great attitude and a smile. If you need to take a vacation from your job, create a strategy to find a new one.

We live in a society with more than seven billion people. As Charlie Munger, the great investor and Warren Buffett's number one guy, said, "To get what you want, you have to deserve what you want. The world is not yet a crazy enough place to reward a whole bunch of undeserving people." You have to put in the time to receive what you want in life by increasing your personal growth.

Working hard is one of the most commonly encouraged traits in podcasts and books. Things don't happen by themselves; they require action. However, not all action pays off. We want things to work out, but when they don't, we get discouraged and want to quit. Moving on with a well-developed strategy will make the difference.

To get past setbacks, you need the right mindset. I have failed at many things, like getting the GRE score I needed to apply to a PhD economics program, but that's fine. Receiving a poor GRE score showed me what I needed to do. Since I was more passionate about starting my business, my wife told me to focus on that rather than retaking the GRE. I'm glad I took her advice because my mindset was to get a PhD in economics and start my business simultaneously. This reminds me of a Confucius quote: "The person who chases two rabbits catches neither." Looking back, I would not have had the capacity to do well in both. I'm glad I chose the business path because I feel like I'm making a bigger impact faster and chasing the right rabbit. Without that failure, I would have traveled a less-rewarding path.

To achieve the right mindset, I try to view failures as experiments. It is important not to dwell on them for too long. What has happened in the past is in the past, and all I can do is move forward.

One of my favorite Tai Lopez podcast episodes is titled "The Four M's of Motivation." He explains that people are usually driven to do things based on money/materialistic things, mastery/status, mating/relationships, and momentum/movement. I feel that I'm motivated by mastery because I constantly want to get better. It is why I read, work out, and say "Yes" to new things. I want to see how far I can go in life.

I grew up in a mobile home, was overweight, and had classmates of all different economic statuses. I knew I could do better in life, and I took action. I joined the Marines because I wanted to be the best and wear the coolest uniforms. I went to school while in the Marines because I wanted to accomplish things faster. I work out because I refuse to be overweight again. I can't stay still and wait for things to come to me.

Motivation by mastery is the main reason I left my secure government job. I didn't want to just show up for a paycheck. I wanted to make a difference. I told my government co-workers that I was going to quit and get an internship at the White House, which I did. I wanted to show people that a person from a small town in Oregon can make it to the White House. If I had relied on eyesight, I would still be living an unfulfilling life in Oregon.

I believe I have the power to change myself through personal growth so I can see increases in my social, economic, and career capital. None of these things would have happened if I hadn't worked hard and deliberately focused on what was necessary to reach my goals.

The Morning Routine That Changed My Life

I discovered *The Miracle Morning* by Hal Elrod because, as a guest on *INspired INsider*, he shared his story about improving himself through the Miracle Morning. This amazing book has greatly increased my morning productivity. Instead of reacting to my day, as I used to, I'm proactive and I dictate what my day will look like.

In *The Miracle Morning*, Elrod encourages six activities that will help you stay focused, balanced, and healthy and that will grow your mind. He uses the acronym "S.A.V.E.R.S":

- **Silent** — Meditating to clear your thoughts
- **Affirmation** — Using positive self-talk to give you confidence about taking on the day
- **Visualization** — Picturing how your day will go and how you will react to the things you plan on doing
- **Exercise** — Taking time to get your heart rate up and give oxygen to your brain
- **Reading** — Reading something for self-improvement (such as the books I've been describing)
- **Scribing** — Writing your thoughts in a journal

For me, scribing is the most important of the six morning rituals because it helps maintain a positive attitude. Every day, I like to write three things I'm grateful for, a small victory I had the day before, and three things I need to accomplish that day. These activities, which take about an hour and a half, fall into the category of important but not urgent.

In my morning routine, I wake up and go to the gym. I ride the stationary bike for 30 minutes, and while I'm on the bike, I write the three things I am grateful for, read a book on professional/personal development, do my affirmations, practice my visualization, and study Spanish. These activities are crucial to my development, and I do them all at the gym in the morning.

I highly recommend that you buy *The Miracle Morning* and listen to Elrod's podcast. It changed my life, and it prompted me to write this book. I especially like *The Miracle Morning* because following S.A.V.E.R.S. brings one percent improvement each day, which is much more manageable than a mindset of fifty or even ten percent. If you take life one day at a time, you can make serious changes in just a year. Consider the power of compound interest. If you start at a baseline of 100 points, getting one percent better for 365 days, at the end of the year, you won't be 365 percent better but over 3,750 percent better. I can't afford *not* to improve 3,750 percent as a person.

Everything you do should be about moving toward the best possible version of yourself. I want this for myself and those around me, and I can only attain it by consistently improving. If I hadn't initially sought self-improvement, I would still be living in Oregon, working at the same grocery store. That is not the life for me.

Setting up Routines for Success

A solid foundation of good habits is the first step toward mastery of a topic or field. It is critical to adopt the necessary behaviors and habits to achieve greatness. Essentially, this means you must adopt habits that help you achieve your goals.

In the book *The ONE Thing,* Gary Keller explains that future goals are not created by chance but by habit. This statement is very powerful because I truly believe the majority of circumstances in your life are and will be dependent on the type of person you are and how you act. Keller also says to take your income and double or triple it. The number doesn't really matter, but the one thing you must ask yourself is, "If I continue as I am, will my income reach that level within the next five years?" If you don't see yourself attaining that goal, you need to think about adopting new habits.

Going from zero to one hundred can be very hard if you don't design your life for success. Keller explains that the right environment is crucial for success. If you spread yourself too thin, you risk failing and are more likely to quit. When it comes to being in alignment, both your mindset and your environment must be in order.

In the book *Switch: How to Change Things When Change Is Hard*, Chip Heath and Dan Heath explain that behavior has a three-part process. The "rider," which is the prefrontal cortex of the brain, is responsible for logical thinking and maintaining self-control, while the "elephant" (the amygdala) is responsible for emotional and instinctive thinking. Then there is the "path," which is environment. If all three parts are in sync, we are more likely to achieve our goals. But if these parts are not in sync, the elephant will do what it wants to do; it is designed to merely survive and use the least amount of energy possible.

The environment — the path — is the most important because it is the easiest to work on immediately. The rider and elephant can be trained to a new way of thinking with enough reps and sets. Most of the environment is about removing distractions that prevent you from focusing on what will take you to the next level. A big part of this is saying "No" to things that will not get you to your goals. This takes practice; you might even have to temporarily configure a new way to achieve your goals because saying "No" can be uncomfortable.

The Easiest Thing to Do — Get Distracted

The easiest thing to do as a human is get distracted. Your attention is constantly diverted by your phone, by your television, at events, through interaction with friends and family, and by a simple walk down the street. In the book *The 7 Habits of Highly Effective People*, Stephen Covey talks about the four quadrants of time management. He explains that each person spends time doing things that are urgent but important, not urgent but important, urgent but not important, and not urgent and not important.

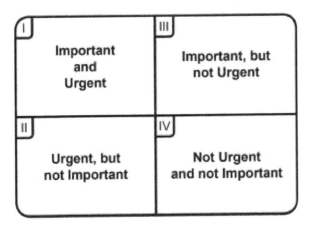

Source: Stephen Covey, 7 Habits of Highly Effective People

You need to spend the majority of your time doing things that are not urgent but important (quadrant three). These things allow growth and self-improvement. If you start to neglect things that are not urgent but important, those things fall into the urgent and important quadrant but become more expensive. Exercise is important, but it is not urgent, and if you neglect this quadrant, you will see diminished performance in your life. This could result in an outcome such as a heart attack that is financially, socially, and mentally expensive. A heart attack will also put extra stress on your family. Reading, writing, planning, building relationships with loved ones, and focusing on your health are also important but not urgent. When you spend your time in quadrant three, you will live a better life. Most people will be distracted by the other quadrants, but you need to be aware and have the discipline to pull yourself back into quadrant three. By focusing on growing myself by staying in quadrant three over the last four years, I feel ten times better and excited about what the future will bring.

For better visualization of this concept, I recommend Jordan Belfort's YouTube video *The 10 Reasons Most People Are Broke*. This video has saved me from doing things that are not in my best interest. Even though Belfort is not the best overall role model, you can still learn from him — both what to do and what not to do. In the video, he discusses the following lessons:
10)

10) **People are unable to manage their state.** You need to see things for what they are, not worse than they are.

9) **They set impotent goals.** Most people settle for mediocrity and comfortable goals. Set goals that are uncomfortable but not unrealistic.

8) **They subscribe to "the secret".** You have to take action and not just believe that things will come to you.

7) **They have limiting beliefs about life and money.** Most people believe life happens to them instead of believing they happen to life. They settle for what life gives and play the victim card.

6) **They choose bad mentors.** To be successful, find a person you can learn from.

5) **They're controlled by fear.** This is the most disempowering state for gaining wealth. You need an achiever mentality to overcome this fear.

4) **They try to reinvent the wheel.** Find a proven system that works and don't stray from it.

3) **They're lousy at business.** Business is not a skill you're born with; it's something you acquire, and it's crucial to learn the language.

2) **They're uncomfortable with words like "sales" and "persuasion".** We're all salesmen because we have to sell ourselves, our ideas, our concepts, and our reasons to others. To get the life you want, you have to become an effective persuader

1) **They slave their lives away for a paycheck.** Don't trade your time for money, but don't quit your day job before you're able to move on.

This is an awesome video because I believe self-control, being growth oriented, and action are key to a good life. Take Belfort's advice: increase your risk tolerance for loss. My risk tolerance for business is high because I left my government job to pursue a career that starts at a low salary, but I believe my choice will provide a very rewarding life down the road. Belfort talks about what it takes to give yourself a life of abundance. My favorite line from the video is "The only thing standing between you and your goal is the bullshit story you keep telling yourself as to why you can't achieve it." This quote represents people who get distracted and don't take the responsibility to improve their lives. Distractions are all around, and it's up to you to deal with them. If you can master this, you will make it much farther in life than most.

To stay in quadrant III, it is really important that you learn how to say "No" because your time is valuable. Once it has been used, you'll never get it back. This is why I am dedicated to the Low Information Diet and avoid watching the news. I don't really know what is going on in the world when it comes to pop culture and politics, but I can give you some tips to improve your life from the books I read. You also have to learn how to say "No" to the distractions in the second quadrant: your smartphone, friends, family, work, or other things. For tips on how to say "No," I recommend James Altucher's podcast on the power of "No." What you focus on is what you will become. A lot of my focus goes into building my business and myself because that keeps me in quadrant III and will help me live the lifestyle I desire and create a positive change in this world.

In the books *The ONE Thing* by Gary Keller and *Deep Work* by Cal Newport, the authors talk about the importance of laser-like focus. Fortunately, we can learn to focus to help us stay in quadrant III. It's like training a muscle that gets stronger with practice. You can do a lot if you sit down and focus your time. I was able to write this book by dedicating four hours each week to write four pages. It took five months to finish the rough draft, but I was able to do it by focusing my attention on what was important to me. Focus on things like reading, working out, and general overall maintenance. Do what is important. Setting up the environment is crucial to helping you correctly focus your time. Quiet places will work better than noisy places, and locking your smartphone in the closet is better than having it right in front of you.

Selling my television and Playstation™ was one of the best things I did to prevent distractions. By removing these objects from my environment, I limited my options for distractions. I fill my time with reading, working, seeing friends, and playing chess. Les Brown said it best: "Turn off your TV and turn on your life!"

This outlook has really helped me do more with my life because I'm not glued to the television. A main indicator of success is how much television you watch on a weekly basis. By removing ten hours of television from my life, I have ten hours to do something else. I now spend that time on more productive activities that will help me grow as a person. Get rid of the television and focus on growing yourself.

Sometimes you need to deal with distractions by rewarding yourself for completing a task. The podcast *Freakonomics* talks a lot about how we can use behavioral economics to trick our brains into doing something and not letting ourselves get distracted. One of my favorite *Freakonomics* episodes is on temptation bundling, which teaches you how to use your guilty pleasures to better yourself. (http://freakonomics.com/podcast/when-willpower-isnt-enough-a-new-freakonomics-radio-podcast/). In temptation bundling, we pair a task that we're not excited about with something we *are* excited about. I usually fold clothes while listening to a podcast. Other people iron while watching television. Instead of being distracted by the television, pair it up with a necessary activity to make yourself better for the future.

Temptation bundling should only be applied to shallow thinking tasks. These are tasks that are monotonous and do not require judgement or critical thinking. Cleaning, cooking, and other light administrative tasks benefit greatly from temptation bundling. You can greatly increase your productivity without feeling like you missed out on your favorite thing. This can be especially helpful during a workout. When I go to the gym, I read a book for 30 minutes and practice my Spanish with Duolingo for 15 minutes while on the stationary bike. Then I listen to a podcast while doing resistance training. This is temptation bundling at its best. You can fit 48 hours' worth of stuff into 24 hours if you bundle your tasks right.

Tasks like studying for the GRE, writing papers, and doing homework require deep thinking and are not suitable for temptation bundling. You have to schedule time to focus on these activities. The book *Deep Work* by Cal Newport will help you realize the importance of working without distractions and focusing on tasks that will help you improve. I've been using this concept to write my book. You have 24 hours in each day — the same as everyone else. You just need to be efficient with your time and work on things that will help you become a better person. As Eric Thomas has talked about in various YouTube videos, if I look at your 24 hours, it will tell me how successful you will be. Be effective with your 24 hours; don't waste them.

It helps to have an environment that keeps you focused and productive as you conduct your deep work. A quiet room with few or no interruptions is key. As Newport says, not all work environments are suitable for deep work, but there are workarounds. It is best to set up a routine in which you do the same task over and over again at the same time each day. This will help you create the behavior and outcome you want. To write this book, I allocated four one-hour sessions per week solely for writing. This deep work helped me become a better writer, and I was able to finish my book in a timely matter.

If two people are studying chess for one hour and one is focused solely on studying while the other allows distractions, the more efficient person will be the better chess player. That person did more with the hour than the distracted person. When working on a task, the easiest thing to do is to allow distractions. When we hear phone notifications, we get a rush of dopamine that makes us feel good when we check our phones[2]. Multitasking is not very effective for productivity.

Think of two cars traveling 500 miles. The first car is cruising on a highway with no traffic, while the second car is in stop-and-go traffic. The second car speeds up and slows down, which is "switching tasks." This car will use up more fuel and take longer to go the 500 miles. Newport explains that when we switch tasks, we are left with a mental residue; we are still thinking about the previous task. I highly recommend Newport's *Deep Work* to help you understand why it is important to have deep focus sessions to reduce distractions and accomplish serious work.

Being efficient is key to getting more done in less time. Strive to make the least amount of moves necessary to accomplish any task. Time-blocking (scheduling your week) on your calendar is one way to be efficient with your time. On Fridays, you should have a general understanding of how next week will look. This will allow you to know when you have meetings, activities, training, etc. It's also important to schedule your important but not urgent tasks. This can be phone calls, practicing a speech, submitting your business expenses, etc. Understanding what you have to do each day is key to being productive. You want to be proactive to your day, not reactive. Thinking about what to do in the immediate present brings trouble. Taking ten minutes to write down your

---

2   McKinsey Quarterly – Recovering from information overload

schedule and review what you have to do the next day or week will save a lot of time. This is why a routine is so powerful. Instead of thinking, you can just *do*.

I don't always have the best habits because life happens and my elephant gets the best of me. Before I go to bed, I like to reflect on what happened during the day and see if I'm moving in the right direction. If not, I know I need to change my environment. This is why writing down your goals is important. Have something to remind you why you are doing the things you do; review your goals often to see if you're on track. In my public health courses, I learned that habits are the key to creating a desired outcome, and we have to be sure to make it as easy as possible to maintain them. I have don't have unlimited willpower to overcome the elephant in every situation, but I can strive to create an environment that best enables me to do so.

The Only Vehicle That Will Carry You through Life

To commit to healthy activities, most people need to make them habits so they don't have to think much about doing them. Although habits don't require much thought, they require willpower — having control over one's behavior. This is crucial to maintaining a healthy lifestyle because many temptations exist that can cause lapses in healthy behavior. Your body is your only vehicle to carry you through life, so taking care of it is extremely important. Attaining a healthy lifestyle is very simple, but it can be difficult to stay on track. Three of the best books I have read about learning to create healthy behaviors are *The Power of Habit* by Charles Duhigg, *Switch: How to Change Things When Change Is Hard* by Chip Heath and Dan Heath, and *The Marshmallow Test* by Walter Mischel. When it comes down to it, it's all about self-control: the ability to delay instant gratification for a bigger goal down the line. These books give insight on self-control and how to manipulate your mind and environment for success.

The biggest takeaway from these books is the fact that self-control is a diminishing habit; your ability to use it becomes harder with each use. This is why people who are exhausted at the end of the day have little self-control; their instinctual habits are to seek sugar or use as little energy as possible, while their self-control is nowhere to be found. When you use a lot of willpower to overcome a temptation, the next temptation will be harder to overcome because your willpower diminished. Try to make a plan to confront your temptations — such as having a healthy snack available at work — so that you need as little willpower as possible. Making plans is crucial for establishing new habits because if you go into a situation unprepared, you will likely fail.

The best way to overcome diminishing self-control is through controlling your environment and putting healthy habits on autopilot. This means keeping certain foods out of the house and making sure the right foods are available. If driving to the gym seems difficult, have exercise equipment at home and know what and when your workout is going to be. This will help reduce the amount of willpower you need to use. According to the Transtheoretical Model, it takes up to six months to maintain a new habit, and forming one is an uphill battle for most. If you can make exercise or healthy eating a habit, you will be happier and more successful in reaching your goals.

To form a workout plan, I suggest you follow FitnessBlender and Blogilates on YouTube or hire a fitness coach. Running on the treadmill is fine, but it is important to also do strength training to keep in balance. During my time as a personal trainer, I realized that most people don't work out all parts of the body; many neglect the hamstrings, glutes, and lower back, which make up the posterior chain of the body and affect basic mobility. On YouTube, I recommend following Bret Contreras for posterior body exercises and Kelly Starrett for tips on how to improve your mobility.

When it comes to eating, I developed healthy eating habits by making a grocery list and preparing delicious healthy meals my wife discovered on Pinterest. Pinterest is the easiest platform for finding brilliant ideas, especially when it comes to delicious food. Trust me: If you want to find a delicious Indian dish to make, Pinterest should be the first site you search. When you find things that peak your interest, pin them to a certain category that you can reference in the future.

Maintaining health can vary greatly for each person, so experiment to see what works for you. I like to go to the gym five to six times a week for an hour for a mixture of cardio and resistance training. Exercising gives me the energy I need to accomplish my day. When I don't exercise, I feel more sluggish and less optimistic. Neglecting exercise and diet is one of the easiest things to do, but you have to make it a priority. Both your body and mind will benefit. Top performers focus on their health; so should you. I also discovered the Jawbone UP fitness band, which helps monitor my exercise, sleep, and food — it tells me how many steps I take, how many hours of sleep I get, how many calories I burn from exercising, and how many calories I consume. This objective view of my habits helps me reach my goals.

I find sleep to be very important. To improve your sleep, I recommend that you follow Shawn Stevenson's podcast and read his book, *Sleep Smarter*. Sleep is important for recovery, maintaining a good memory, and maintaining overall good health. I find that in order to do the Miracle Morning properly, you need a good pre-bedtime routine. To make tomorrow successful, prepare today. There is nothing better than waking up refreshed and ready to take on the day. Read *Sleep Smarter* for more sleeping hacks to help you live a better life.

One of the best sleep tips from the book to is to wear orange-tinted glasses 30 minutes before you go to bed. The glasses block out the blue light emitted from your smartphone or television screen, which disrupts the sleep-enhancing melatonin production in your body. (This makes sense because a blue sky typically means that it is day time.) Because of orange-tinted glasses and blackout curtains, I typically fall asleep pretty quickly when I shut off the lights. Blackout curtains are also important for sleep because your body has detectors that sense light and keep you awake if there is a light source near you. I get some of the best sleep at hotels because the rooms are cool (human bodies like to sleep at 75 degrees) and the curtains block out all light. I recently discovered f.lux for my laptop and Twilight for my Android smartphone. By giving my screens an orange hue, these programs gradually remove the blue light from my screens the closer I get to bedtime.

With a good night's sleep, I am more likely to remember things, I have more energy, and people don't remark that I look tired. I try to hit eight hours each night, but sometimes I do have to take a cat nap. I like being a financial advisor because my Outlook calendar dictates my day. If I don't have an appointment and I'm feeling tired, I take a nap, especially after I eat lunch and need a break. If I can squeeze in 15 minutes, I'm fine. Naps are awesome and help me stay refreshed for what the rest of the day brings.

Getting a good night's sleep is one of the most important things you can do for yourself. Stevenson explains that when you get only six hours of sleep, the part of your brain responsible for logical thinking (the prefrontal cortex) will decrease its operational capacity by 14 percent. To become the best, I have to be in peak shape, so I can't afford to be operating at 86 percent.

I also find that preparing my lunch and laying out my clothes the night before makes it much easier to wake up. Instead of thinking, I just react. When I wake up, it takes me awhile to get going. If I don't have my things ready the night before, I am more likely to forget something when I leave. I'm not one to wake up just to wake up. I need a reason to get up. I try to get to the gym between 6:15 and 6:30. This fitness goal is important to motivate me to go to bed early and get up in the morning. Exercising in the morning instead of at night is also helpful for falling asleep faster and more soundly because your body's temperature is higher after you work out, and a hot body has a harder time falling asleep. Just another reason to get your workout done first thing in the morning.

Stress can be a huge drain on willpower reserves when it comes to eating right and exercising. When I was working full time and going to school, exercising and healthy eating were usually compromised. It was hard to come home late and make a healthy meal when I was exhausted.

You can overcome this by making one big meal to eat over several days and choosing healthier options when eating out. If you are too busy or stressed to exercise, you can get exercise in different ways. Try parking at the end of a parking lot instead of near a store's entrance, taking stairs instead of elevators, and taking walking breaks at work. When I use public transportation, I like to get off one stop before my destination so I have to walk a few extra blocks. This can add 10–15 minutes of walking, but I gain valuable exercise. Strive to walk around 10,000 steps a day, which is about 5 miles. (This does not have to be done all at once.)

It is wise to start a new exercise or diet plan when you have the least amount of stress in your life because you will be more likely to succeed. If you have a lapse in your diet or exercise routine, tomorrow is a new day. Willpower usually regenerates each day — it is strongest in the morning and weakest at night. If exercising at night is tough, try to exercise in the morning or at lunch. To minimize the temptation to eat something unhealthy, eat breakfast at home and bring a lunch to work.

If you follow these tips for maintaining willpower, exercise and diet should become easier. Missing a week of exercising or eating poorly over a weekend shouldn't discourage you into abandoning your healthy behaviors. You simply had a lapse in judgment, or the options for success weren't available. Things come up, but tomorrow is a new day.

You must have the right fuel and maintain your body for success. Your body is the only vehicle you have to drive you through life. You can operate as a Bugatti or as a 20-year-old pickup truck on its last good month. Take care of your body and it will take care of you.

The Mind Follows the Body and the Body Follows the Mind

Proper body posture is crucial for confidence. Good posture can improve your mood and decrease pain. When I took the ACE Personal Trainer Certification, I learned the qualities of good posture. Since I used to be a personal trainer, I like to observe people's feet, hips, and shoulders for deficiencies. Many people tend to walk duck-footed, round and hunch their shoulders, and tilt their hips forward.

Working out is crucial for maintaining good posture. Aside from the fact that I was a Marine, my workouts are the reason I have so much energy and good posture. I would not be able to function every day at 100 miles per hour if I didn't work out. Staying active will help you stay positive. In addition, I know I have to work out all areas of my body to remain in balance. I recommend going to a personal trainer that knows GAIT. You will be shown areas that need improvement and given exercises to work on. I also recommend taking yoga classes for stretching.

In the book *The Charisma Myth*, Olivia Cabane warns against walking with crossed arms, and she recommends walking as though a string is pulling on the top of your head to help you walk taller. You want your body language to send the message that you are not closed off and that you're willing to be approached. It's best to leave your hands out of your pockets, hanging by your side. Also, do not slouch when you sit. Tell your friends and family to call you out if you're exhibiting bad posture.

When it comes to changing your mood, I highly recommend that you smile more. People like it when you approach them with a smile instead of a neutral face. If you bring energy with your smile, people are more likely to help you out. I would rather deal with smiling people than people who look like they want to fight. In *How to Win Friends and Influence People*, Dale Carnegie describes smiling and calling people by their first names as one of the central ways to get people to open up to you. They will be more likely to trust you.

So brush your teeth and get ready to smile at people. It might take some effort, but move through your day thinking of things that make you laugh. At work, I walk around with a smile all day and say "Hi" to my co-workers. I want to be a positive influence on their lives, not a negative one. Have a good attitude because your reactions can affect those in your workplace. If you don't like something, fake it until you leave or address the issue.

Strive to leave a positive impact in all areas of your life. Don't offer a negative attitude. Change has to start with you, not the other way around. Make sure you have your body posture in line and a smile on your face. The mind follows the body and the body follows the mind. Every time you go through a room, check to make sure you have positive body language. Stay aware and don't get complacent. You can improve if you focus.

Goals Don't Happen by Accident

Figure out what you want from life and go for it. In the book *Never Eat Alone*, Keith Ferrazzi explains that people seek three things in life for happiness: wealth, health, and family. By focusing on bettering yourself through various sources of knowledge, you are more likely to achieve your goals in these areas. Goals don't happen by accident. You must have a purpose and execute wisely, without worry of failure. Things happen, and failure is just a signal that you need to try again or work on something that will help you succeed down the road. The internet can provide a lot of knowledge on how to prevent failure, but choosing a good strategy is even more important. A mentor can help you choose.

Since you won't achieve your goals by accident, it is important to execute on a strategy and a plan. The execution phase of your life will be a lifelong journey because the world is constantly changing, but it is changing for the good. I don't like to think of life as a zero-sum game. There will not be just one winner and one loser with only so much to go around. As humans, we have the ability to grow our resources and come together to make things better. Continue to work on yourself and your team because, as Tai Lopez says, time and decay go in the same direction. If you don't put any energy into yourself or your team, you will decay and become non-functional or non-existent.

Many people don't put effort into improving their situation. I find it shocking that 60 percent of college graduates never read another book after graduation. Again, some people think that things are good enough and that the world will not change without them. But it will change — with or without you — and you will be left behind, wondering why things didn't work out.

I also find it upsetting that only seven percent of people like listening to motivational programs. These programs put me in control of my spirit for the day. A mindset that enables you to execute the steps to accomplish your goals is crucial, and listening to motivational programs works for me. If they don't work for you, try to find something else.

One key to positive change is not only hard work but *deliberate* hard work. Each person has 24 hours in each day, but some of us are more intentional with our time than others. I love how Les Brown says, "If you go through life being casual, you will end up a casualty." I recommend a great YouTube video called *Are You Hungry?* It is a 10-minute mash-up from Brown's 45-minute video called *You Gotta Be Hungry*. In a great trend on YouTube, speeches are being condensed into mash-ups. A lot of people are jumping on this bandwagon, and I hope it doesn't stop.

The main theme for many of these mash-ups is hard work. Without hard work, plans are just dreams. In *So Good They Can't Ignore You*, Cal Newport goes into detail on this subject. He explains that to result in greatness, your hard work must have substance and strategy.

I wish I had read this book back in 2013 because I committed a violation of one of the rules — don't leave your job unless you have the career capital to make a living and people who will pay you. I thought I could just leave my job at the Pentagon and start making a living as a health coach. However, I should have become a personal trainer instead. I thought the path of a health coach was good because I studied public health in school, and we focused heavily on behavior change. The first indication that I had made the wrong move came when I was practicing my coaching skills on my wife and only offering health advice. She asked, "That's all you're doing?" I realized that I needed to add the personal training component so I could give people more than just words and stop expecting them to know what to do. It was a good life lesson on understanding the market audience. However, spending $12 for Newport's *So Good They Can't Ignore You* e-book, taking three hours to read the book, and asking people for feedback would have been easier than spending $500 on a health coaching course and three months studying for the exam.

In *So Good They Can't Ignore You*, Newport explains that you need career capital so you can have more control over your life. When you have more career capital people will care about what you do. Career capital equals control because people demand your services, and this allows you the luxury of choosing what to do. I had no career capital when I started as a health coach, so I decided to become a certified personal trainer and started working at a gym. During this process, I also decided to take a TRX course and a kettlebell course, which helped me become an even better personal trainer.

These courses have reaped many rewards for me following my time as a personal trainer. Now as a financial advisor I use my personal training skills to connect with people. To build rapport and improve my social network, I routinely invite people to work out. I decided to leave personal training because I believed I could make a bigger difference as a financial advisor. I started a company called The Wealth and Health Coach, but I quickly realized that I could only focus my time as a financial advisor. To live the good life where you have health, wealth, and family, you have to be willing to take action, learn along the way, and have patience.

One of the best lessons I've learned from a book is in *Never Eat Alone*. Keith Ferrazzi explains that "no one becomes an astronaut by accident." I take this to mean that we have to be intentional with our lives. I don't expect anything to come my way, and I will continue to work hard to attain the good life.

Be deliberate in what you do each day. The majority of your actions should be in line with becoming your "astronaut." In my day-to-day job as a financial advisor, I am deliberate about becoming a master in financial planning by studying new materials and getting in front of other people. Many people are not intentional with their days. They take life as it comes, and this mindset prevents them from becoming their "astronaut". By reading Ferrazzi's book, you will learn about the journey to becoming intentional. It requires effort, but you will live a much better life in the end. Understand your goals, then develop a strategy and a plan to work toward those goals. A great strategy to help me reach my goals is to create a checklist for the items I need to complete for the day. I learned this from my mom who always kept a checklist when I was growing up. Using this method has helped me stay deliberate in what I do each day. Instead of a scrap piece of paper like my mom, I use Evernote to keep track of my checklist and I love how I can check it on my laptop and phone. If you don't have a checklist, then how can you know for sure what you need to do with your day?

One of my goals is to speak Spanish. I'm intentional in this by incorporating it into my workout routine. Through the Duolingo app, I practice for 15 minutes while riding the stationary bike. Practicing 15 minutes each day is 7.5 hours more per month than I used to practice. I spend the rest of the time on the bike reading a book that will help me with personal development. This helps me reach my goal of reading 36 books each year.

These goals will help me become a better person because I'm deliberate. A goal is only as good as its plan and execution. Many people just wish and hope for change, but you have to get out and work. Some people say that wishing takes the same amount of energy as planning, but you shouldn't have to wish for anything because most things in life don't happen by accident.

Stay deliberate. I find it easiest to work on my goals in the morning. In my schedule, I only have time in the morning to do things that are important but not urgent. No one will interrupt me, and I'm not likely to be distracted. I find that my morning routine of riding the stationary bike and doing the Miracle Morning is perfect for me. This requires work, but you have to build the habit and be committed to the process. When I look back on each month, I should see that I am a better person than when the month started. This is how all of life should be. Nothing upsets me more than wasted potential.

I grew up in a lower-income socioeconomic status in a mixed-income community, and I saw others who had more than I had even though I worked harder. However, I think it was good to grow up in this situation because it made me hungry to do better and achieve more. I didn't have it rough as a child, but I had to be deliberate, patient, and industrious in pursuing and obtaining my goals. I like to think that I have the growth mindset — I believe I can outgrow any situation by being deliberate in my actions.

Another way I stay deliberate is by sticking to my calendar. My calendar is everything to me. It tells me where to go, what to do, and who I need to see. Thank God for smartphones, because I could not do as much as I do without mine. Learning how to use your smartphone effectively is key to staying productive and deliberate. Just make sure you don't put anything distracting on your phone. Being intentional is necessary for growth. It's fine to take time to rest and avoid thinking, but don't overdo it.

Les Brown say is, "If you can't see the future you want, you can and should create it." This takes me back to high school. I knew I wanted to do better in life and I knew education was key, but I didn't have money or scholarships. So I joined the Marine Corps to obtain the G.I. Bill. Typically the G.I. Bill is used by veterans when they leave the service, but the 36 months of benefits it provides is enough for a bachelor's degree if it is used right. However, another educational benefit called tuition assistance is available for those in active duty. Tuition assistance provides $4500 per fiscal year, enough for about six to eight classes per year. Some of my fellow Marines, now that they are out, regret not taking advantage of tuition assistance because their G.I. Bill benefits ran out. Since I did take advantage of tuition of assistance to load up on college credits while on active duty, I now have two bachelor's degrees and will soon have an MBA paid for, all because I was intentional about obtaining my education goals. I refused to settle for the life I was given and let opportunities pass because I knew I could control my outcome.

From this experience, I know I can never be complacent. I never want to fall behind. Self-improvement is dear to me because as I grew up, I could have wished to have the good life, but I also knew that the good life was more likely to happen if I became a better person. I'm an opportunity seeker, and I know I have to be prepared. When you're passionate about something and working on that goal, you will constantly wish for more time. I am amazed by the amount of work it takes to start a business. Since I started as a financial advisor, I have yet to look at the clock and wish it was a certain time in the future. I love that my career has given me this mindset, and this is a byproduct of living a deliberate life. There is so much to do and not enough time to do it all, so each day I make an effort to focus on the three most important things I need to do.

Another amazing thing about being deliberate in obtaining my goals is that I'm rarely bored. I constantly have things to do and I'm optimizing my day for success. I'm excited for the future because I'm accumulating a lot of skills for future opportunities.

My dad was intentional in seeking a better life. Growing up poor in a small village in Oaxaca, Mexico, he knew that moving to the United States would create a better life. I'm thankful he came because I'm here today to benefit from his hard work and sacrifice. He could have thought it was not fair to cross the border, but he just did what he needed to do to make his goals happen. Like my father, I want to create my future and pursue my goals. I am really good at planning and executing. I'm not so great at the creative stuff, but if you need a plan and want that plan to be executed, I'm your man.

If you're like me, you'll try to go out and create something that will make society better. By mastering Spanish, I hope to be able to help a whole new population better themselves. I feel that Latinos are distinctly underrepresented in various professional fields. In the financial services sector, Latinos only comprise about five percent of the workforce. This is a big problem for the Latino community because an understanding of the language of money is necessary for a high level of success. This is why I love my job so much — I get to help professional Latinos make a financial difference in their lives. When I speak Spanish fluently, I will be able to reach an entire different population and create the change I want to see in the world.

So go out in the world and create your life. You have to be intentional and work very hard, but it will eventually pay off. I will continue to be deliberate in my life because I think the world will benefit.

Go Inch by Inch and It Will Be a Cinch

When we're looking to improve, we should not try to go from zero to one hundred overnight. An inexperienced driver who does this will most likely wreck the car. A large part of success is about making constant incremental progress. Les Brown said it best: "If we go by the yard, it's hard, but by inch by inch, it will be a cinch." I don't believe everything in life will go by the inch, but moving slowly provides more opportunities to attain that yard. Life tends to be unforgiving towards people seeking immediate huge gains. Go after progress and you'll make it in no time.

However, sometimes it will take a long, long time to reach your desired level of success. As Les Brown says, success is like the bamboo nut — to grow, it requires five years of daily watering and fertilization. If one day is skipped, the bamboo nut will perish. But once the seal is cracked, the bamboo tree will grow 60 feet in 90 days. Most people will say it took 90 days to grow 60 feet, but in reality, it took 5 years and 90 days. It's this type of incremental progress that will help you grow exponentially.

Most people are loss averse: they hate losing twice as much as they like winning. To progress in life, you have to accept some losses. If you never fail, it is because you never really try or give much effort. Effort, not talent, causes people to become great. To become great, you have to put in the 10,000 hours of deliberate practice. In addition, you are more valuable if you hustle with a great attitude but have only mediocre skills than if you have talent but a poor attitude.

If you haven't watched Steve Jobs' Stanford commencement speech, take some time out of your day to watch or listen to it. The biggest take-away is that you can't connect the dots forwards, only backwards. To attain success, Steve Jobs had to do certain things in life. He failed out of Reed College but hung around college anyway. He received inspiration from a calligraphy class and wanted to make beautifully designed products. He also was adopted by parents that cared for him, and friends like Steve Wozniak helped him on his long journey.

Where you are now is based on what happened in your past. The more you did to help yourself grow as a person in the past, the more opportunities you'll have today. To grow as a person, you must actively seek to learn. The more you learn, the more you earn, but this will take time. Be patient and just get one percent better every day.

How to Grow the Pie, Not Just Divide It into More Slices

As Aristotle said, "The whole is greater than the sum of its parts." When we focus on growing mentally, physically, and spiritually, we can make society a better place through our improved skills. When we become better professionals, we can do more in less time, which frees us to do other things. Then, when we trade our skills with other professionals, we can accomplish even more.

Being a great professional does not involve a "winner-takes-all" environment. This really only applies to competitions like sports. In the book *Bounce*, Matthew Syed discusses the fact that although many people strive to become great athletes, only one winner can take home the championship. However, if a doctor becomes the best in his field, he is able to see more clients, provide better diagnoses, and give more work to people like nurses and administrators. Society is better off as a result because wait times are reduced and clients recover faster, which allows them to return to work faster and be productive members of society.

Society is counting on us. This is why it is so important to grow ourselves. When it comes to business in the United States, there is no zero-sum game. If you work hard to improve your skills through purposeful practice, you can make many things happen. In *Bounce*, Syed describes the many tedious hours and sacrifices various experts put into their craft to become successful. These depictions are not glorious, but if you want to become great in your field, the components described are necessary.

My two and your two can equal something more than four if we bring the right twos to the table. Be a good person, show the world you're worth something, and seek to interact with people who will help you do great things together. I feel like many people have the "scarcity mentality" that makes them more selfish in certain areas of their life than they should be. This is not the right way to perceive things. It is better to have the "growth mindset"; if one opportunity doesn't work out, another is waiting for you if you stay in the game. People need to think like Richard Branson and know that another opportunity bus will come by in fifteen minutes.

In order to have this "whole is greater than the sum of its parts" society, we need to build our skills. In *Bounce* by Matthew Syed and *So Good They Can't Ignore You* by Cal Newport, the authors discuss deliberate practice. If one person plays pick-up basketball while another works on certain skills with a coach, the latter will most likely turn out better because learning requires feedback. Without feedback, people continue in bad habits and work inefficiently. Being deliberate instead of casual will help you become a better person. We must put in the 10,000 hours of practice and be purposeful about it. Society has come a long way over the past 200 years because productivity advances have caused us to do more with fewer resources and in less time. In my opinion, today is the best time to be alive, but there are more distractions than ever to keep people off the path toward greatness.

Allocate time to focus on improving yourself. Being great requires action, and we must just get started. I hear a lot of excuses that prevent people from starting to build the foundation for their lives: "I don't have time," "I have too much work," "I have some other things going on," etc. I usually ask, "How is that going for you?" For the most part, people simply live the same lives they lived five years ago.

Again, to accomplish things, you must take action. If you choose the wrong action, at least you will know what not to do again. You have to be like Thomas Edison and Lewis Latimer, who went through thousands of filaments to make the lightbulb. Persistence matters more than being a genius and doing something right the first time.

One of the best things you can do is hire a coach or mentor to give you feedback. I strongly believe that you cannot learn without feedback. Feedback can be uncomfortable at times; you don't want to be embarrassed in front of your peers. Always seek feedback because you can't learn without it. You need someone to coach you — to explain what you're doing right and which areas you can improve. Feedback is crucial right off the bat because it can prevent you from wasting a lot of time. If you have a co-worker, have him critique you. If you don't have a co-worker, ask a friend or family member, or even better, hire a coach. Coaches are professionals that know what to look for and how to use their experience to help you improve. You don't always find the answer from within. As Tai Lopez says, you find it externally. One way to do this is by seeking feedback.

This is why I decided to take my first coaching session in 2016 with *The Art of Charm*. People often balk at buying things like coaching sessions. No one wants to hand over money without receiving a value that exceeds the price. But someone competent can provide significant feedback to make you a better person. To become the best person possible, I allocate at least three percent of my salary to self-improvement, including conferences, seminars, books, and courses. By taking these measures, I'm changing my energy from a flashlight to a laser, and I'm using my mindset to make it happen.

Seek to Be Corrected or You'll Never Learn

I used to hate writing. I usually just wrote papers and turned them in without proofreading them. Naturally, I received awful grades. Teachers told me to proofread my papers, but I never did. My wife changed this fault in me. When I sent her my first paper to proofread, she slayed me for my poor grammar and lack of proofreading. I thought I was just a bad writer, but with enough practice, I eventually improved. Now I'm writing a book! The biggest step I took was following the feedback from my wife. I began reading my sentences out loud and reviewing my papers three or four times before sending them to her. Now when I ask people to review my papers, I receive much better feedback on content rather than grammar. I now also have the ability to review papers for other people. Thank God for my wife's feedback because without it, I wouldn't be writing this book and sharing my skills with the world.

Improving as a financial advisor requires a lot of practice and feedback. This can be uncomfortable, but it is worth it.

When you receive constructive feedback, cherish the lessons you learn. Many things go unchecked because people are not comfortable making corrections or seeking feedback. However, feedback from a professional eye is key because it can help you avoid many things you may unknowingly be doing wrong.

When I was a personal trainer, one of the best things I did professionally was take a kettlebell and TRX course from instructors who sought to improve the profession. I was able to learn new materials, and I became a much better personal trainer. Learn from someone who is passionate about his profession and makes suggestions on how to improve the industry.

When you are corrected and become better the second time around, your confidence will be boosted and the intensity will increase. We are not perfect human beings; every area of our lives can be improved. You have to be comfortable with making mistakes. No one has ever been born to do something. People who are good at what they do have simply put in more practice than others. People are deficient in parts of their lives because they don't want to look like a fool and are afraid of failure. I still get this feeling, but it is lessening with time. The best thing to do is just say, "Fuck it, let's do it." Ask your spouse or significant other to give you feedback. I routinely do this. At the office, I ask colleagues to help me with issues or to listen to my pitch. I receive a lot of great feedback from their critiques.

If you work in a dynamic environment, such as sales, in which you deal with many different people, seek various critics to help you prepare for the different situations you might come across. Also, try to ask people three things you did right, three areas you can improve, and three things you should remove. If you don't have access to outside critique, try videotaping or voice recording yourself to get personal feedback.

Feedback has to be comprehensive. You can't focus solely on the good or the bad feedback. You need to focus on both if you want to make it far. You don't need a drill instructor like I endured in the Marines, but, as I said earlier, you will have to do what's uncomfortable. You have to be comfortable being uncomfortable. This is one of the best lessons you can take with you and teach others.

In *Bounce*, Syed says that feedback is crucial for progress. If you swing a club and don't understand what causes the ball to go straight, you're setting yourself up for failure. You have to understand why you do or do not reach your goals. Edison was a master at this because when something didn't go right, he took that feedback as a sign that things wouldn't work out and tried something new.

Most people receive feedback but are not willing to do what is necessary to implement that feedback. You must be willing to make yourself vulnerable and be critiqued. If you're trying to lose weight, going to the gym might be a good way for you to meet that goal. However, if you don't lose the weight after going to the gym, you probably need an outside source to give you feedback. You might not be eating correctly or sleeping enough. You also might not be working out hard enough. When I go to the gym, I see many people not pushing themselves to get better. They just coast through the workout, not receiving as large a benefit from their time at the gym as they could.

Finding someone to keep you accountable is crucial to helping you get one percent better every day. Writing things down will help you stay focused. Journaling and using a priority list will help you identify what objectives you need to accomplish. If you want to see how to use your time better, I recommend using a Gantt chart. I have one on my website, Growwithjoe.me, that you can download.

You can lay out what you need to do for the day, and a pie chart will show you how your day was spent. You might be wasting your time on a lot of little things that prevent you from accomplishing big things.

To learn how to properly focus, I highly recommend that you read *The ONE Thing* by Gary Keller. This book will help you understand why it is so important to focus on the one thing that will make everything else in your life easier. Some people use an hour better than others. You can make another dollar, but you can't make another hour. In economics classes, you're told that time is the scarcest resource, so make sure you don't waste it.

Motivational speaker Eric Thomas is adamant about using time wisely. As you can see in his YouTube video *Secrets to Success, How Bad Do you Want it,* he stresses that people use their cell phones too much and watch too much television. Thomas also tells stories of athletes not wanting to party because they practice ten times more than everyone else to become a success. You can't grow yourself and become more productive if you're constantly distracted.

Use this time management advice to grow as a person. However, to grow, you need to take the time to learn and practice your skill. In a few months or years, you will receive feedback from your actions. Not everything is immediate; feedback takes time. It takes 6 months to build a Rolls Royce but 13 hours to create a Toyota. Do you want to be mediocre or do you want to be great? Ask yourself, "Am I doing the right things to give myself a better future?" If not, use that feedback to make a change in your life so you don't have to live a life you already want to change.

I am not a big fan of work-life balance because it takes a lot of time to become an expert in a field. Just figure out what you want in life and go after it. If your desire is to have a family, pursue that. My goal is to become the best version of myself, which will allow me to help others in a great capacity but give me control over my day. This is where I put a majority of my time and effort, and I love it.

Everything You Do Should Be Based on Value, Not What's Good or Bad

As a high school graduate, I filled out various college applications and was accepted to several schools, but when I realized the costs involved, I thought, "How am I supposed to pay for all this?" I joined the Marine Corps primarily to get paid, take advantage of tuition assistance, and utilize the G.I. Bill when I finished serving after four years. It was one of the best decisions of my life because I met a lot of interesting people, was paid to go to school, and was led to a life I never knew could exist. Things were not perfect, but I was able to accomplish my main goal — a college education.

While studying economics, I learned that creating an options list directly correlates with opportunity costs (the costs of the action you choose not to do in order to perform your chosen action). For example, if you choose to watch an hour of television, your opportunity cost is one hour of study time, which may result in a bad grade on your exam if you haven't studied at all. On the flipside, by watching television instead of studying, you may give yourself a chance to relax after already studying for three hours.

Most decisions, such as considering whether or not to go to college, require deep thought. Most people don't have the knowledge or wisdom to make such decisions, and it is important to get opinions from outside sources. That's why reading, listening to podcasts, and watching YouTube videos have been so powerful for me. For the most part, I know what I want out of life and what I have to do to get it, but this knowledge came from a lot of learning from outside sources. I know which resources I need to go after and who I need to talk to. This isn't a quick ride, but that's the fun part. The stories are not in the destination; they are in the journey. Your life story shouldn't have an ending until it's over. It should only have progress markers to show where you were and where you are now.

There is a great article titled "After the Gold: Olympic Medalists Struggle With Life" by Brian Alexander that explains that some Olympic athletes can fall into depression, drug abuse, and commit suicide after they retire from their sport. Some see the Olympic Games as an endpoint and miss the high that competing in the Olympics gives them and then can't manage their lives afterwards. For these Olympic athletes, they peak in their 20's and then it's hard to figure out where to go next. I saw this same outcome with Marines getting out of the Marine Corps because they lack a sense of purpose when they get out and either want to get back in, lead a destructive life, or figure out a way to pivot to something meaningful for themselves. Sometimes people ask me if I miss the Marine Corps and I usually tell them no because I've been constantly working on myself since I got out and I love the progress I've made since I left active duty in 2011. I don't want past events to be the apex of my life, I want them to be progress markers to see how far I made it. I see life continually getting better because I'm getting better.

When developing your life, choose the options that fit your life, will give you the most flexibility down the line, and offer the biggest long-term return on happiness. I'm all about progress, and when it came down to choosing between my home state of Oregon and Washington, D.C., I opted for D.C. The decision has really paid off because I have been able to do things I could never do in Oregon.

Making your options list can be really scary. Quitting your job and starting a business is quite a risk. The options from a successful business sound great, but massive action is required. In 2013, I asked myself this question: Do I want to keep this stable government job in which I have little control, little creativity, and no autonomy, or do I want to start an unstable career that that will offer all those things and eventually provide more money than my bosses make? I am not one to settle for mediocrity, so staying in my federal job wasn't going to satisfy me. Ultimately, you need to decide what you're willing to deal with and do to create the life you want. I work a lot of hours, sometimes for little pay, but this is very much worth it to me compared to the alternative because I know my future options.

In addition, I think people need to be more careful when deciding which college to attend. As I pursue my MBA, I plan to go to the school that provides the biggest benefit and costs the least. If attending Harvard would result in a 10X return, I would consider the option. However, I don't see that happening for me. Most of the time, your ability as a person is much more valued than where you went to school. In D.C., I see people who went to Ivy League schools in the same positions as people who went to state schools. The common trait is the same — they are motivated and willing to work hard.

Figure out what you want to do in life, then try to spend the least amount of resources to obtain those goals. This is not a one-size-fits-all plan, but if life doesn't work out as planned, you can take actions to get back on track.

To help you accomplish the scary goals that offer high rewards, I suggest you watch Steve Harvey's *You Have to Jump?* on YouTube. This motivating five-minute video describes the value of jumping and trusting that your "parachute" will open. If you never take the chance to go after that promotion, start that business, or ask that girl out, you'll never get to experience what life has to offer and will live in dissatisfaction. Harvey explains that you will feel uncomfortable when you take your jump because you'll be vulnerable, but eventually your parachute will open.

I highly recommend that you watch this video as soon as possible so you can actively pursue your goals. Loss aversion is something that I think holds a lot of people back: they are too afraid of losing something, like their job that offers a modest salary. But as Harvey says in the video, if you don't jump and pursue a career that offers financial independence, "you won't be able to afford anything anyway." See what your options are in life, and if you don't like them, find something that will change them for the better. I wrote this book because I believe it will give me options that I wouldn't have had otherwise. This book might not become a success, but I will feel accomplished for simply starting, sticking to the process, staying disciplined over the long haul, and putting my wisdom on paper so others can enjoy it.

Following your options list will probably lead to the most successful methods of self-improvement. If you suggest this concept to others, they will probably choose the safer but mediocre option. Ask them, "How is that working out for you?" See if they realize they should probably pursue the riskier but more rewarding option.

Don't Get Stuck; Have Flexibility and Control

It is important to have flexibility and control in your life. As I explained earlier, Tai Lopez says it correctly: You should make an options list instead of a pros and cons list. Then, go with the option that will give you the most flexibility and control over future situations. The last thing you want is to be forever stuck in a situation. The choices you make today will determine future outcomes, so focus on making decisions that offer freedom.

For example, exercise is a pretty good everyday choice. The long-term benefits of exercising daily will give you flexibility and control of your future self. Instead of being stuck in your home with mobility issues in your 60's and 70's, you can have a much more active lifestyle. Once you choose to exercise routinely, you can learn techniques to improve your overall efficiency. These include a good diet, stretching, weight training, and good sleeping habits. Watching an extra hour of television might be more enjoyable than going for a walk or to the gym, but it won't provide long-term benefits and might bind you in a situation you won't want in the future.

To determine which options will give you flexibility and control, you need experience and knowledge. For most of my life, I had neither, so I didn't know what options to take. However, I tried different things. Now that I'm in my 30's and have experienced life in the military, as a federal employee, as a service employee, and now as a business owner, I have a pretty good sense of what I want. In addition, with all the new people I meet and the knowledge I consume, I am able to shape the direction I'm headed. Now I know which event I should attend, what course I should take, and what my day-to-day activities should be. As you grow older and obtain more experience, you tend to better understand the opportunity costs of your decisions. As a kid and young adult, I spent a lot of time watching television and playing video games and didn't fully optimize my days because I didn't know what I wanted to do. Joining the Marines after graduating from high school was the event that helped lead me to better decisions.

Don't worry if every decision you make doesn't fully optimize your day or your future life. Life is filled with uncertainty, and some decisions won't have a major impact. Also, don't feel like you have to constantly work. If you need to take a break, take a break. Sharpening the saw if it becomes dull will help you become more productive in the future. If the majority of options you take are good, you won't have to worry about getting stuck in the long run.

Since every decision you make won't go 100 percent your way, it is important to initially do as little as possible to make things work out. The book *The $100 Startup* by Chris Guillebeau relays stories of people who maximized their current options to take on a much more interesting life. They delivered products or services with the least amount of resources or put out minimal viable product (MVP). *The $100 Startup* is a good read for people who want to change careers. It offers great lessons to help individuals decide whether or not to leap into a new adventure. One story describes a man who was fired from his sales job and then started a mattress business because a friend had extra mattresses to sell. To store the mattresses, he rented an old building that had been a used car dealership and, via Craigslist, he sold the mattresses. His business became successful because he was creative in marketing the business and didn't use a lot of resources to start it. I made many mistakes in my business by buying things or spending a lot of time on tasks that provided little value. If I had taken the MVP route, I would have saved a lot of time and money.

Since personal finance interested me, I decided to become a financial advisor. I like to analyze a person's overall financial picture and come up with a strategy and plan to help him or her reach a higher level. Many times I wanted to quit because things seemed so overwhelming and were not going as well as I wanted. It would have been easier to make $50K to $60K each year at a decent financial analyst job in the Washington, D.C. area. However, this option wouldn't have allowed me to make the impact I want to make in life nor given me progress in myself and my business. I'm living the life I want to live; becoming a financial advisor was the right option for me.

We tend to get better at the things we focus on — the option we've currently chosen. If you only focus your attention on television, you'll be really good at watching television. However, there is probably not a bright future in this, so it's better to direct your attention on things that will improve you. This is why I put so much attention on learning and gaining knowledge — these give me the most flexibility and control.

I have chosen the wrong option at times, but I don't really dwell on the past. Ruminating on the result of a decision or what you missed in the past is bad for you. Perceive those events objectively and use them as learning opportunities to help guide your life. Just move on.

When you make your options list, try to focus on just two or three. As Tim Ferriss says, if everything is important, nothing is important. Instead of feeling pressured into many different things and stressing yourself out, you can be more at peace by optimizing those two or three options. As Tai Lopez would say, you don't need to complete everything in one day; you just need to optimize the day.

To do this, decide which options will give you the most flexibility and control, then delegate the other stuff if you can. If you spend four hours each day focusing on the important stuff, you will get one percent better. Spend five to ten minutes to plan out the next day and write down the top three things you need to accomplish. If you get those items done, you can take time to enjoy the rest of your day. If you don't finish those items, that's fine, also, because you will have a clearer idea of what to do the next day. We only have one life, so instead of thinking it is short and feeling stuck, let's do the things that will make it feel long and give us the control and flexibility we want.

Grow by Being Uncomfortable

To grow in life — to accomplish many great things — you have to accept discomfort. This mindset will become easier with time and practice. In the book *Relentless: From Good to Great to Unstoppable,* Tim Grover explains that many athletes choose to do intense workouts and play through injuries to accomplish their dreams of winning a championship. Grover says that it takes a certain type of person to work this way. He calls these people "cleaners." Cleaners are able to do what it takes to make things happen. They don't have excuses; they just do. They are also unconditionally rude to people who get in the way or tell them something is impossible. To become a Michael Jordan or a Kobe Bryant — to work in a winner-takes-all environment and leave a legacy — you have to become a cleaner. You don't have to reach the level of Michael Jordan or Kobe Bryant, but you will need to endure uncomfortable events and be mentally strong in order to grow yourself.

In *Deep Work,* Cal Newport talks about the importance of focusing on a subject for four uninterrupted hours. (This can be especially tough for people who have to check their phones every time a notification pops up.) In the book, Newport tells a story of a guy who quit his job as a financial analyst to go back to his parents' basement and study code. He spent ten-hour days improving his skill set. After three months, he completed a short but intensive computer programming course to help him change careers as a competent computer programmer. Since he knew how to do deep work by pushing through his comfort zone, he succeeded while other students suffered or failed. All that deep work eventually paid off because he is now paid good money to do something he wants to do. He learned how to be comfortable with being uncomfortable when others couldn't handle the intense computer programming course.

Deciding to quit my job as a federal employee was very uncomfortable at first. I had to tell my wife that I wanted to quit, and then I had to tell my bosses. I knew I would lose my benefits and miss a promotion in six months, but I had to pursue something more fulfilling. Looking back, overcoming these uncomfortable times really paid off. I'm in a career that I love, and I'm much happier as a person. It's a lot more work, but I enjoy it. I can't really think of one thing that was initially uncomfortable that ended up bad. In most cases, these uncomfortable situations provided a life lesson, some new-found confidence, or something I really desired.

Sometimes people delay doing something hard because they don't think they're ready to take the next step. To overcome this type of discomfort, I recommend a great episode called "iProcrastinate" on *The Art of Charm* podcast. The biggest takeaway is that "you don't have to be great to get started; you just have to get started to become great." Too often, we let our present selves detract from our future selves by allowing ourselves to be comfortable with our current situation and never take the uncomfortable first steps to pursuing our goals. It can be hard to do things that are uncomfortable, but you need repeated exposure to those uncomfortable events to get desensitized. Sometimes that just means getting up from your comfort zone and trying.

Learning to be comfortable with being uncomfortable is one of the most useful lessons you can learn. I am not perfect, and the issue with being uncomfortable is that you set yourself up for vulnerability and possible failure. It sucks to feel this way, but most of the time, those vulnerabilities are not that bad. Enduring the uncomfortable moments can lead to some of the biggest leaps in progress. As recommended by *The Art of Charm*, I have been trying to do more uncomfortable things, such as communicating my feelings with my wife, and I've seen a positive difference. I was told that if I do something uncomfortable every day, I will be a better person. To fulfill this goal, I take a 30-second cold shower. This is uncomfortable, but I feel better after doing it. It makes me realize that I can do something uncomfortable and still survive. Strive to do one uncomfortable thing per day and you will grow one percent better.

There Will Always Be an Obstacle; Go Overcome It

As individuals, we face and will continue to face many obstacles. Life is not one smooth journey. I heard on a podcast that the average millionaire will face bankruptcy 3.1 times and that, on average, some type of disaster will occur every 90 days for every person. These can be financial, family, work, or social disasters — things that will disrupt your flow and potentially dampen or ruin your day. Dealing with these obstacles is crucial for success and growth opportunities. When faced with an obstacle you cannot say, "That's it. I'm done." You have to be creative with that obstacle, deal with it, and be prepared for another.

One of the best lessons I learned in high school was from the book *Fahrenheit 451* by Ray Bradbury — you can't have good days without bad days. Difficult situations are part of nature, which means you're dealing with variables you can't control. Don't freak out. Be prepared.

A great book that deals with obstacles is *The Obstacle Is the Way* by Ryan Holiday. This is one of the top ten books you should read because of its great stories. I especially like how every chapter is a clear-cut lesson. Holiday tells of famous people who overcame obstacles, breaking down those experiences into three phases.

1. **You have to perceive the obstacle the right way** — take action against that obstacle and have the will to endure it. People who overcome obstacles perceive them as objectively as possible. They understand that there are no good or bad events; there are just events. How we perceive and deal with those events will determine what we get out of them. People who take a subjective approach, imagining events are too difficult and involved, are more likely to see the object as unattainable and complain or have a lot of anxiety. Instead of panicking, maintain the right mindset and a cool head. You will go much further.

2. **When you have an obstacle, you must take action**, which will lead to more action. Most people fail in life because when they see an obstacle, their momentum decreases. To succeed, you have to create a system of constant, persistent action. The last two years of my life have been all about action because my goals require massive action. In addition, being disciplined will help you stay on the course. Your body and mind will want to take the easy way out, but you just need to keep moving forward.

3. **You must have a will.** Intrinsic motivation will help you stay on course when everything around you is going astray. Accepting what happens and believing in the process of action will help you get by. Thomas Edison's factory burned down when he was 65, but he grew excited and told his family that it was the greatest thing to happen because they would never again see a fire that big. Even though he lost many important things in the fire, such as documents and equipment, Edison ended up earning even greater profits the following years. You must prepare to start again because bad circumstances will come your way, and you will have to deal with them.

On his Snapchat, Tai Lopez says that he uses $100 bills as bookmarks because he knows that money can be made from reading books. I agree with him, and it is pretty sad that most people are not learning and growing as they should. This is what *The Obstacle Is the Way* is all about — learning from the obstacles then growing into a better person who then typically earns more. I wish I had known these lessons earlier in life, but I have the next 40 or more years to work on my craft. I don't want to wake up one day and say "Dang, my life sucks, I don't like where I'm at right now, and I'm too stuck in my ways to change anything." I can't be ordinary because ordinary doesn't bring progress. I love how I have been able to overcome obstacles and pursue the life I want — not someone else's life; my life. Oh, it has been stressful, but at least it is for me. I'm doing more than I ever thought I could be doing, and I attribute that success to reading books like *The Obstacle Is the Way*.

This book is a must-read. In the back, Holiday explains that Marcus Aurelius and Epictetus greatly influenced the book. Those authors and the stoic philosophy seemed to hugely influence many prominent people, such as George Washington and Tim Ferris. I was so motivated by what I read in *The Obstacle Is the Way* that I immediately bought *Meditations* by Marcus Aurelius and read it within a week. Books like these make me want to find other great books because they put me in the right mindset, I can use the information immediately, and they are great to share with others.

Meditations is about stoicism — the endurance of pain or hardship without complaint and how to not let your ego get in the way. Many things will go wrong in your life, and how you react will determine the outcome. Feelings come from within, and you can react positively or a negatively.

Marcus Aurelius explained that internally you can handle many things, but you can't really control what life gives you[3]. Things will go wrong, and you can complain or you can rise above your emotions and see everything from an objective point of view. He also expressed that we should be good people through and through. You can control whether or not you are good, and you should ignore what others say about you.

---

3   http://99u.com/articles/24401/a-makers-guidebook-9-stoic-principles-to-nurture-your-life-and-work

You can accomplish a lot in life if you aren't held back by your emotions, feelings of discomfort, or pain. Negative events will happen, and you have to deal with them.

I also like the message in *Meditations* that you should live your life and not fear death. Everyone has a finite amount of time left and should make the best of it. The best way to live is to focus on growing yourself and making a difference. As Les Brown says,

> "The graveyard is the richest place on earth, because it is here that you will find all the hopes and dreams that were never fulfilled, the books that were never written, the songs that were never sung, the inventions that were never shared, the cures that were never discovered, all because someone was too afraid to take that first step, keep with the problem, or determined to carry out their dream."

Don't be the person on his deathbed who wishes he had more time. If your time has come, just embrace it, as Marcus Aurelius would have. A life of regret is worse than death. You don't want to look back on your life someday and say, "I wish I had more time." You only get the time allotted to you; that's how nature rolls.

I like how Marcus Aurelius explained that nature will react but that it's up to us to react in turn and deal with what nature sends. Your mindset is your most powerful tool. If you think the right way, you can deal with many things in life. This is why I read so much — it puts my mindset in the right place and helps me focus on positive things. I don't like listening to the radio or watching television because there is a lot of negativity out there. Reading a book like *Meditations* helps me have a mindset of achievement and overcoming obstacles.

Bad things will happen in your life, and you will have to deal with them. These can be awful things like tearing your ACL on the second day of football practice or getting into a serious car accident. I have personally dealt with these issues, but there will be someone else in society that will face much worse. When terrible things happen, we should offer support to those experiencing those things, but we must learn how to move past them in our own lives and move forward. I used to focus a lot on the past and "should have" or "could have" situations, but I'm different now because of books like *Meditations*. I don't focus much on past incidents unless I'm affected by them in the present or will be affected in the future. For the most part, these are just events, and I need to take action and move forward.

Just deal with each present situation — be a good person, be humble, put in effort, and try to learn what you can do better the next time a bad situation comes around. Once you start thinking like this, life will become much more satisfying and less stressful. Instead of worrying about things out of your control, focus on the action you can take to improve a situation.

After reading *Meditations*, I can certainly understand why it is a favorite of big-time CEOs and other influencers that focus on leadership. Bill Clinton says it is his favorite book and reads it every year. A future goal of mine is to take reading vacations for a weekend — to just read in nature, finish three books, and write down what I learned.

I highly recommend *Meditations*; it will change your mindset. People who accomplish things take action and happen to life instead of letting life happen to them. One of my wife's favorite quotes is "Done is better than perfect" from Sakita Holley in the podcast *Hashtags and Stilettos*. This is a good reminder to take action in spite of fear. I plan to re-read *Meditations* and take notes because if leaders like Tim Ferris praise this book, I have social proof that I need to do the same.

Things You Can and Cannot Control

In life, there are things you can control and things you can't. The way that you perceive these things will have a dramatic effect on your life. I was told that you should write things you can control on one piece of paper and things you can't control on another piece of paper. Then throw the paper of things you can't control in the trash. Stop wasting your time on these things, such as what other people do, how a sports team performs, or what nature sends your way. This will ward off a lot of stress and will help you live more calmly.

As a reminder, there are no good or bad events, there are just events. How you deal with those events will have a big impact on how they play out in your life. To learn more about how to perceive events, listen to episode 287 on *The Art of Charm* podcast. Hunter Maats does a great job explaining how to come up with different stories on how to explain each event we come across. He gives the example of someone cutting you off in traffic. You could get mad at the event that you have no control over, but it's unlikely that you'll get revenge. Conversely, you could picture a parent trying to rush his sick kid to the doctor. The second scenario will more likely put you in a calm state of mind than thinking the driver is an asshole and doesn't know how to drive. You can't control the driver, but you can control how you think about things.

I sprained my knee in March of 2016, and I could've sulked for weeks that I missed out on running my half marathon and the Cherry Blossom Ten Mile Run, but I saw it as a chance to improve myself in other areas. One thing that really helps me stay in a positive mindset is writing down three things I'm grateful for every day. Even on my worst days, I can think of things that make me grateful for where I am.

When it comes to allocating your attention, focus on the things you can control and forget the rest. Don't use up your expensive attention span. Time — your attention — is the scarcest resource because once you use it up, it is gone forever. Time only moves forward. If you're in a sales position like I am, you can only focus on the inputs like calls and e-mails sent out, people met, and meetings scheduled. You can't really focus on the outcomes like people who didn't answer and people who rescheduled meetings. It's okay, however, because you can find something else to fill those vacant spots. As Tai Lopez always says, if you're good at something and you can control it, double down on that activity.

In areas you can't control, be diverse because things can go wrong. Have a varied group of friends because if someone is out of town or a lot of people are busy, you will still have someone to hang out with. When it comes to your life, you can't control how every part of it will turn out, so it's important to be diversified by gaining wisdom and learning new skills.

Being diversified provides a buffer to soften the blow against setbacks. Animals need biodiversity to protect themselves against disease. It is recommended that at least 50 different members of a species live in a geographic area to mate with each other to lessen their chance of getting wiped out by one disease. Again, if you can't control something, diversify. When life happens, you'll be better prepared. I'm working on getting seven sources of income because if one of my sources goes awry, I'll have six more to depend on. I'm seeking seven sources because that is the average number of sources a millionaire has. Like I said, success leaves a trail you can follow. I can't completely control what happens to my sources of income, so I'm going to diversify.

When something does go wrong, you need to have the mental strength to continue and let go of the event if it is out of your control. Not dwelling on things that are out of your control will prevent a lot of chronic stress in your life. Chronic stress is very harmful to the body, and if you let it into your life, you're just digging an early grave. If you accept the thing that didn't go your way or find a solution to prevent it in the future, you'll live a good life.

Success Leaves a Trail

I strongly believe that success leaves trails. Great leaders drop wisdom that you can pick up to help you change your life.

Evan Carmichael has put out a good series on YouTube called *Top 10 Rules for Success*. This video series shows how certain people obtained success and includes their 10 rules of success. Carmichael does a great job combining various video clips into a nice 10- to 15-minute video. I also like how he places each rule of success on the side of each video as it plays. I also recommend the Oprah and Eric Thomas videos by Evan Carmichael. They are motivating and offer great tips. As you watch, I suggest that you write in your notebook how you can apply and implement the rules of success. The biggest thing that people are missing in their lives is execution.

Eric Thomas' ten rules for success are:

1. **Know what you want**
   Each one of us can listen to Eric Thomas' message and receive inspiration about the next steps we should take. Personally, I want to be the best financial advisor possible and inspire other Latinos to build their wealth. Financial planning, patience, and persistence are my gifts, and these are great traits to have as a financial advisor.

2. **Work on your gift**

   I work on my gift by practicing my speeches and talking to other financial advisors when I have problems solving clients' issues. I also plan to get my CFP® in 2018 and start my MBA program in 2017. If you want to be so good that people can't ignore you, you must focus on your gifts and be a known expert in your field.

3. **No excuses**

   People don't want to hear your excuses; they just want you to do what you say you're going to do.

4. **Upgrade your values**

   When you raise your standard, your standard of living goes up. Far too many people have standards that are too low and a lifestyle that shows it. Upgrading your values requires a lot of work, and it's not always easy to stay on track, but high standards will set you apart from the rest.

5. **You reap what you sow**

   For me, this means understanding that I must continue to improve my craft as a financial advisor in order to get the reward I want out of life. I might not get everything right away, but I'm making connections with people and putting in the work to be known as a great financial advisor. It takes a while, but because of the work I put into my craft, it will be worth it in the end.

6. **Education is the great equalizer**

   Education is a big part of my life. It's the reason I read 36 books each year and listen to many podcasts. It gives me a slight advantage over other people.

7. **What is your "why"?**

   Knowing your "why" is important and will help you move towards your goals by mindsight and not by eyesight.

8. **Have boundaries**

   Boundaries are important for success. If you keep getting interrupted, you mess up your flow and can't accomplish the things to help you reach your goals. Remember the great Confucius saying: "The person who chases two rabbits catches neither." Stay focused on your one rabbit and keep within that boundary.

9. **Speak from the heart**

Speaking from the heart is also important because it demonstrates your passion and gives other people a reason to like and believe in you. I find that I am able to connect with people on a deeper level when I tell them why I became a financial advisor.

10. **Succeed as bad as you want to breathe**

Number ten is probably the most important. If you haven't heard Eric Thomas' "Succeed as bad as you want to breathe" speech, check it out. I can tell myself I want to succeed as badly as I want to breathe, but my actions must prove it. It will be painful and hard, but I know I can make it to another level through hard work, planning, and execution. For the past year, I worked nearly every day to make my dream a reality. I want it so badly that I'm willing to avoid things that are unimportant and don't fit within my goals. Rule number ten is, in my opinion, the one rule you *must* follow. You have to want your goal and have a strategy and a plan to help you achieve it. Having a burning desire will help you stick with the plan and strategy as life tries to pull you away from your dream. This is why wanting success as badly as you want to breathe will help you achieve that next level.

I love what I do, and I want my dream badly enough that I'm willing to make sacrifices to make it happen. Watching the *Top 10 Rules for Success* series serves as a reminder for why I am following my path to my goals and gives me tips on how I can achieve them faster.

Fuck It, Let's Do It

Joining the Marines was a very positive point in my life. I met many great people and had many life changing experiences. One of my favorite sayings is "Fuck it, let's do it," which I learned from my Marine Corps buddy David De La Rosa. I was very timid about doing things, but he was a very "let's go do it" kind of guy. If we were dragging our feet about some task, he would say, "Fuuuuuck it, let's do it." Now, whenever I am reluctant to do something, I just say, "Fuck it, let's do it." Action is very important. When I say, "Fuck it, let's do it," I know I'm ready to start. It releases everything that is holding me back.

De La Rosa was also responsible for helping me start my Roth IRA when I was 19 because of his "Fuck it, let's do it" mentality. This was one of the best decisions I've ever made, and I want to thank him for it.

In *The Seven Levels of Communication*, Michael Maher says people should say, "Do it now" 50 times each day. I didn't find this very helpful but, "Fuck it, let's do it" takes me back to my Marine Corps days. I guess I just built the habit of saying it. Do whatever works best for you. It doesn't really matter if it's "Do it now," "Fuck it, let's do it," or "Just do it." It's better than saying, "Oh, let's wait," "I'll do it tomorrow," "I'll do it later," "I can't do that yet," or whatever mindset is preventing you from taking action.

Whether you do a task now or in the future, the same amount of energy is required. The only difference is that if you do it now, you open yourself to another option or opportunity much sooner. By doing things now, you are gulping life instead of sipping it. When you gulp life, you will get a lot more out of it, so put yourself in the right mental state for getting stuff done.

For me, saying, "Fuck it, let's do it" brings motivation. It's like in the movie "Captain America: Civil War," when Bucky is told those sayings from the journal and becomes an assassin. We're creatures of habit, and if you have a saying that keeps your focus aligned and helps you achieve your goals, use those words. I have pretty good self-control, but I do get distracted from time to time, and saying these words puts me back into focus. I usually say them in my head, but it helps to say them out loud every once in a while. Saying the phrase in a confident manner can also make your friends laugh.

Taking action is crucial. Don't be like the 95 percent of people who let life or perfection get in the way. If you know 75 percent of the material, take the leap because most successful people run a ship held together by duct tape.

To start this career as a financial advisor, I really had to say "Fuck it, let's do it" and stop working at a stable, secure job. There was a huge learning curve, and I had to say "Fuck it, let's do it" to keep going. I'm still operating under this mentality because it helps me to take action when action is needed.

You will have two outcomes: Your goal will turn out well or it will turn into an opportunity for learning. View failure as an experiment to analyze a situation and see how you can improve, or just take it as a loss and seek to improve on the next opportunity. Not everything will go right, but you have to try in order to have success. The "Fuck it, let's do it" mentality helps you do things you don't want to do or are afraid of doing.

I find it especially helpful when I'm exercising. When I'm exhausted and don't want to move forward, I just say "Fuck it, let's do it," and I am able to go through the routine. My old lifting partner, Rob, used to laugh because I would say, "I don't want to do this, I don't want to do this, fuck it, let's do it" and actually go through the exercise routine. I did my exercise and pushed myself to new limits with this method. So if you find yourself not wanting to go, use this phrase or something similar. Thank God I met De La Rosa because he gave me the mindset I needed to do things. It was a slow process, and it wasn't until several years later that those words really sank in. I've always liked executing, and using those words help me do the things I need to do to be successful.

I also like to say "Fuck it" or "Fuck it, man" in a relaxed manner as a way to let go of anything stressful that I can't control, such as when my car was broken into. I simply had to deal with the situation. When I say those words, I am accepting what happened and moving forward.

Hal Elrod has a good tip called the "five-minute rule," which allows five minutes for dwelling on something. After that, you have to let go. So bust out your smartphone and get the timer ready because you only have five minutes to brood. Once that timer rings, you should say those magic words — "Fuck it" — and move on if it is something you can't control. This takes practice and belief in the system.

So the next time you need to speak in front of a group, talk to your boss, or do something uncomfortable, just say "Fuck it, let's do it" and take action. This system will help you stay on course and reach your goals. Not doing something usually brings regret, and dwelling on your lack of desire will only increase your stress levels. If you prevent these attitudes, you will usually be better off.

Executing is where most people fall short. Life is all about executing, executing, and more executing. I believe it is better to accomplish 75 percent of something than to wait for all the pieces to fall in place. There will never be a perfect time to do something. Start off slowly if you need to, but the key is to just do something.

Professionals Stick to a Schedule; Amateurs Let Life Get in the Way

When it comes to executing, you have to act like a professional. Professionals put in the time and practice and have the discipline to follow their goals. Far too many people don't put in this effort. In any occupation, you can see who is willing to do the work and who isn't. I want to deal with professionals that have the grit and persistence to make great things happen. I would choose someone who hustles over someone who is talented any day.

You really have to be selfish with your time. If you have extraordinary goals, you must do extraordinary things to achieve them. You won't achieve them if you live a casual life. This might mean waking up early in the morning so no one interrupts you. Instead of going out with your friends, work on a project that will take you to the next level. It might even cause you to say "No" to family events. As Jordan Harbinger said, "Professionals stick to the schedule; amateurs let life get in the way." All ultra-successful people focus on things that help them become successful.

I remember a time when someone came into my office to pitch his service. Being in the sales industry myself, I know what to look for in a pitch. This guy was not prepared. He was reading off his slides, and his words did not come off effortlessly. He had obviously not practiced his pitch very much, and if he was not serious about his pitch, how could I know he would be serious about providing me with good service? I didn't know him very well, I had never worked with him, and he had not been recommended by anyone I knew. When he asked for the sell, I had to decline because I wasn't convinced about his service. If he had been more of a professional and had practiced his pitch, I might have been convinced.

You don't need to know everything about your product or career, but you must be sure about certain things. If you're giving a presentation with information on each slide, you had better know what it is. It's okay not to know the answer to every question you're asked. You simply have to say "I'm not familiar with that topic, but I can get back to you if you give me your contact information."

I practice my presentations several times until I am confident I will be able to spit back the information to my intended audience. In early 2016, I spent 20 hours preparing for a seminar in which I was going to speak to 30 people; it was my second presentation ever as financial advisor. My mindset is always to do the best job I can, so I practiced hard on my speeches. I was excited because I was set to go first, and I wanted to set the standard. When I gave my pitch, I received a thumbs up from the president of the organization, which made me feel great.

However, the two presentations that followed me were only "okay." This was because the other presenters didn't prepare very much for their presentations, and it showed. I feel that too many people don't put time into their crafts because they let life get in the way. I remember practicing my seminar speech for two hours on a Friday evening because I knew I wanted to do a great job. There is always room for improvement, and I seek constructive criticism so I can implement changes in future seminars. Don't let life get in the way.

When I was the best man at my friend's wedding, my wife told me to practice my toast, and I did. People said I did a good job. The maid of honor didn't practice her toast and basically told the crowd that the bride knew a lot of men in the past. This example is why I practice my presentations over and over again because I don't want to disrespect someone.

Harbinger has a great show because he puts in the time to know his guests and find out what great questions to ask. To be a professional, you need to schedule time to work on your craft. If you put the tasks you need to complete in your Google or Outlook calendar, they are more likely to happen.

If you aren't a professional or working toward becoming one, things can go wrong. You will either not get what you want or embarrass yourself in front of others. It all comes down to practice, practice, and more practice. Professionals put in the time to become experts in their fields, and this causes other people to seek their services. People want to put their faith in someone who will help them out and take care of them, not someone who is careless with time and might make a mistake. Unlike amateurs, professionals stick to the schedule and don't let life get in the way. The difference between the two can be seen in their paychecks and bank statements. Be a professional in everything you do because how you do anything is how you do everything.

But don't take practice too far; you don't have to do everything to perfection. That mindset can really slow you down and keep you from accomplishing things. As Bird Dunn once said, "Perfection is the enemy of completion." If we always had to wait until everything was perfect, we would not get very far. This was one of the downfalls for Germany in World War II. When it came to plane production, they wanted everything to be perfect. The United States' "good enough" approach allowed them to get to the fight quicker.

In my career, where I'm responsible for up to 400 people, it would be impossible to be perfect for each client on my own. This is where efficiency and knowing how to delegate to your team matter. You can't take forever to do a task because there is literally not enough time in the day to get everything done. The most important thing for me is making sure my clients are doing the things they need to do to be successful and that everything is set up for them to do so in the most efficient manner.

Sometimes you actually *need* to take action without a lot of practice because that is what the opportunity calls for. You don't have to be the perfect dancer or perfect speaker to seek an opportunity. You just have to take action. If you want to find a new relationship or business opportunity, hustle and find somebody else who did it first. Taking action and being a professional will take you far in life.

You have to stick to your schedule and not let life interrupt. I want to accomplish huge goals in life, and I need to be a professional to make it all happen. I love this anonymous quote: "Entrepreneurship is living a few years of your life like most people won't so that you can spend the rest of your life like most people can't." Most people don't want to live that professional lifestyle because it is hard and stressful. It can be much easier to throw in the towel and focus on simple tasks like social media or watching television while avoiding the things you need to do to progress.

Sticking to these tasks will require a lot of discipline, and as Harbinger said, "Discipline only matters when it is needed." It is easy to go to the gym after a full night's rest, and it is easy to follow your diet when there is no temptation lying around. But when things go wrong and you're stressed out, you need discipline. This is one of the most realistic things Harbinger says in his podcasts. The best way to build willpower and discipline is to have a burning desire for the task ahead of you. You have to want it so badly that nothing will stop you from accomplishing it. You might have to disappoint some people, but this is for you. You also need to build the habits that will allow discipline to come easier. Be a professional and stick to the schedule. You'll be worth more than the amateur in no time.

Things might suck where you are, but look for opportunities to be a professional. When I was in the Marine Corps, I found these opportunities. I wanted to be color sergeant and present the American flag at events. No one really wanted that title, and I took it and was thanked for my service. My ultimate goal was to present the colors at a Portland Trail Blazers game, but I hurt my back before I could make that dream come true. However, I was able to practice at smaller, more important events like funerals before I hurt my back. These events made the possibility of presenting the colors at events like an NBA game more realistic, and the people in attendance appreciated our professionalism. Being the color sergeant showed me that professionalism is a desired trait and you develop a level of self-satisfaction knowing you did your best. There were times when I dreaded being in the Marine Corps, but I tried to be a professional most of the time, and that made the difficult times easier to deal with because I knew I did a great job.

The lesson I learned about being a professional is one of the great values of being a Marine Corps veteran. What group guards our nation's embassies, is the first to fight, and has a band labeled "The President's Own"? It is the Marines, and it is because we act like professionals.

Through professionalism I have become a better person, and I look forward to becoming even better every day. Professionals learn, seek advice, admit fault, and do the right thing rather than the easy thing. I recommend looking at professionals in your field to see how they think and act. Success leaves trails, and professionals are willing to help others grow.

Please don't confuse this concept with the idea that you need to be an expert to start a new venture. No one knows one hundred percent of the answers because life is so complicated. You do have to be a professional and try your best. If you fail, learn from it and improve the next time you're up to bat.

Professionals recognize professionals, and we would rather be around professionals that make us better. As Erika Bearman says, "If you're the smartest person in the room, you're in the wrong place." You're wasting your time by staying in that room. If you're not the smartest person in the room, be sure to ask questions like "How did that happen?" or "Why did it end up like that?" If someone says he had trouble with a client, I like to ask how or why the client was troublesome and what was done to fix the problem.

Seeking wisdom from others will help you deal with future challenges. Rather than dealing with problems by yourself, learn from the mistakes and challenges of others. This will save you money and time down the line. Seek assistance. Once, when I was having trouble with a particular area at work in which I was not conducting my meetings in a professional manner, I sought training from the training professional at work. I told my colleague my trouble, and with his help, I started seeing a difference when I interacted with clients. Don't be too proud to seek help; you will only do yourself a disservice.

There are ten things you can do that require no talent at all that will help you become a professional:

- Be on time
- Have a great work ethic
- Put in the effort
- Have positive body language
- Have a lot of energy
- Have a great attitude
- Be passionate about what you're doing
- Be coachable
- Go the extra mile
- Be prepared

These require extra energy, but the effort will separate you from the pack. Not trying and doing the bare minimum are recipes for disaster. Success requires effort, no one will come along to make your dreams come true. I don't want to live a mediocre life in which I am dependent on someone else to give me a chance — someone who has the ability to take that chance away from me.

Being a professional will help me achieve my dreams. Successful people don't let life happen to them. They happen to life. As I said, this requires action. We all want to quit at times, but you have to remind yourself why you must keep going.

An episode on *The Art of Charm* describes an amazing story about a girl from India who experienced misfortune after misfortune on her way to becoming a doctor. She even went blind during her first year of medical school. However, she was persistent, had some lucky breaks, and is now a doctor. Life can suck, but you can make the best of it by focusing on the things you can control. You can control those ten points to become a professional. Just don't let life get in the way. Look at your schedule and see where you can become a professional. If you're watching television or spending too much time on your smartphone, replace that activity with something more productive. Locking up my phone and not owning a television forces me to focus on the tasks ahead and continue to work toward my goals.

In his *You Have to Jump* video, Steve Harvey talks about his friend who acted like a professional with his lawn care business by missing social events because he had to wake up early and cut his customers' lawns. For many years, his friends made fun of him for not enjoying his life. However, Steve's friend went on to build a million-dollar business. You can achieve this, too, with hard work, knowledge, and persistence. Make it happen for yourself. Who else will make it happen for you? If you think investing in yourself is not worth it, just wait until you "get the tab for not investing," as the great Jim Rohn says.

One of my favorite ways to build a habit to become a professional is the Chain Method. Go to *The ONE Thing* website, download the template, and write down what habit you are going to do for the next 66 days. There are 66 blocks for you to enter an "X" in. The goal is to get the chain as long as possible. It is very motivating to see the chain four days deep. Jerry Seinfeld is credited for this because he had a goal of writing down one joke each day, and each day he marked the task on a calendar if he accomplished it. I used this method for making phone calls, and it helped keep me going.

It takes time to build up to a strong habit, but you can do it just by getting started. Being intentional about your goals will help you be a professional. There are too many amateurs out there. I love where I am in life because I am a professional and it gives me so much satisfaction.

Never Stop Being a Student

I highly recommend Ryan Holiday's *Top 10 Rules for Success*, compiled by Evan Carmichael. The biggest takeaway is that you should never stop being a student. Students have a mindset of deliberate learning and acquiring knowledge to solve problems.

I have been practicing this principle for the last five years, and it has helped me be more creative in my career. Also, I'm able to give value to other people. I'm in the constant mindset of personal growth, and I'm able to help others grow. I didn't grow up with a privileged life, but I know that by focusing on improving myself by constantly learning and using that knowledge, I can make my life better.

I created a book club on Facebook to give all my friends another opportunity to learn with me. I once read that a good book club has six to eight people, so I shot for that. A book club is a way to meet other people and see how they implement the ideas of the book to better their lives. They might have seen something that I didn't see, and they can share that insight with me. If you're trying to read one book each month, I recommend creating your own book club so you have an opportunity to discuss the books and stay accountable.

One of the other principles of Holiday's talk is to never act like you've "made it." As Rory Vaden said, "Success is never owned; it is only rented — and the rent is due every day." Looking back, I realize that I made a mistake when I first started out as a financial advisor. Things were going really well and I wasn't pushing myself hard enough. Then things started to slow down, and I had to jump through hoops. A lot of people "drop their packs," as we say in the Marine Corps, and start doing the bare minimum. When you do this, you leave yourself open, allowing someone else to take your spot. I also think it causes people underneath you to despise you. I despised some people when I was a federal employee and in the Marine Corps because I saw that they were not pulling their weight and I saw that it was not fair. You have to stay hungry, and this is why it is important to review your goals on a daily basis. It will serve as the compass for your life.

I write my goals in a journal and review them before I go to bed. When you review your goals, think of small action steps you can take during the day to help you get closer to those goals. My daily actions to help me achieve my goals are reading for at least 30 minutes, making phone calls to set up appointments, exercising for an hour, and reviewing my schedule for the following two days. If you live and die by your schedule, I recommend that you look ahead two to three days and confirm with people that they can still make their appointments. If you look ahead only one day, by the time you review your schedule, it might be too late to call. An assistant can be a great help in this.

Seek to get the most out of life and to make it a better place than it was when you entered. I love that there is so much knowledge available to enable me and others to make the world a better place. We just need to grab it and use it. The internet has made the world a better place by allowing society quick access to information, but the successful ones are those who actually implement and execute the information. Knowledge, planning, and execution are major keys to success.

Another thing I like about the *Top 10 Rules for Success* is Holiday's urge to never give up the beginner's mindset, which is like the immigrant's mindset. Get excited about learning something new — soak up new material like a sponge. After a while, you will see improvements in yourself and will be more valuable. This is why I like finding new books and listening to podcasts. Through these avenues, I can expose myself to a variety of professionals. If I like how someone explains his profession on a podcast, I am more likely to purchase his material.

Seeking new material will help you enjoy the process of continual learning because the material will be fresh and won't seem boring. At times you will have to push through some material, but if you have a good process for learning and understand your purpose, the process will be easier. This is why written goals help. Write down a reason for each goal. Many of the reasons behind my goals go back to my parents, my childhood, the change I want to see in the world, my time in the military, and being Latino. Having reasons behind your goals will help you stick with those goals through the rough times. I have the ability to do what I want to do in life because I take action, acknowledge that the rent is due every day, and never stop learning.

Learn like you're going to live forever; you will most likely live a long time. This is why it is important to never stop being a student. Try to get in the habit of writing down ten ideas every day, as James Altucher describes. My ideas are usually tailored to how I can improve my life or business, but I also write ideas for other people. If you have a boss, write down ten ideas for him or her. If your boss doesn't like the ideas, don't take it personally. A lot of my ideas are not the best, but I just look for the few valuable ones. Not all of them have to be used. This is just an exercise in creativity.

As Altucher says, try to mix ideas together to become even more creative. For me, that means mixing my experiences in public health, economics, personal finance, and the books I've read into a new creative idea. If you work at this every day, you'll feel mentally stronger, even if most of your ideas are not that great. We don't rise to our expectations. We fall to our level of training, and being students and strengthening our minds will help us deal with life's challenges and opportunities.

Experiment with Your Life

There is a lot of advice out there, but not everything will fit your personality or body type. This is why experimentation is crucial. Not everything I learn is solid gold, but I have that prospecting mindset. People ask me why I read so many books on the same subject. They think I'm just being repetitive. However, I have found that when I seek different opinions on the same subject, I get a more comprehensive idea of what to do in life. When I get fixated on something, I try to gain as much information on that subject as possible so I can be successful in that area.

I thought I had everything set up to write this book until my friend Rudy introduced me to a book I mentioned earlier — *The $100 Startup* by Chris Guillebeau. It clarified how to get the book marketing process started. I have also received recommendations from friends and other sources. I try to follow the success of others to make my life better in the process.

I like how *The $100 Startup* provides a lot of little stories about people who became successful business owners. Knowledge is power, but acting on that knowledge provides ten times the results if you experiment enough. You can always hire someone to do the work for you, but if you're just starting out, the internet and the library can be your best work partners. Never stop learning and discovering new ways to be successful.

We have to constantly work on ourselves because success is not guaranteed. It might sound exhausting, but if you're progressing and achieving new things, it won't feel like work. Stressful times will come with experimentation, but don't always avoid that stress. Living a complete-ly stress-free life is not a good thing. Stress provides opportunities for growth, and failure is an opportunity for feedback and acquiring wisdom. When you're experimenting, learn to quit something quickly if it is not working. This could be a book you're reading or a podcast you're listening to. After reading *Extreme Productivity* by Robert Pozen, I learned that I didn't need to read all the articles in *The Economist* and that I didn't need to listen to every podcast all the way through. Time is scarce, and not all experiments need to be completed. You may need to cut things from your life that are not important to your goals. Examples include watching excessive television, scrolling social media for hours, getting drunk multiple times per week, play-ing *Candy Crush* all day on your phone — basically anything that will not pro-vide future value. Entertainment is fine in moderation, but make sure you're on track to accomplish your goals and then go have fun.

Far too many people get complacent in their ways, and life passes them by. Again, as Tai Lopez says, time and decay move in the same direction.

If you don't put energy into learning new skills to make yourself bet-ter, you'll be like a rundown house. Simply dedicating one hour each day over five years to your craft will make you a much better person down the line. Gain skills and refine those skills through experimentation. I want to be the best financial advisor I can possibly be. I will do great things in the future because I'm doing great things to improve myself now. You have to put in the work and overcome your fears. Seeking resources and experi-menting will be key to your ongoing success.

Some people are really good at getting a lot done in 24 hours, but others are not. To build your skills in order to get more stuff done, I highly recommend experimenting with task stacking, which combines multiple tasks into one. In contrast to multitasking, task stacking allows you to fill time that would otherwise be spent waiting.

A good example of task stacking is listening to podcasts while you travel to work. Most people commute to work on autopilot and are technically just waiting to get to work. Why not focus your attention on something that will make you better? It takes me about 30 minutes to get to work, so instead of listening to music, I listen to a podcast that will help me. When I am waiting for an appointment, I usually read a book or play chess on my phone instead of looking at Facebook.

Your time is finite, so you have to be selfish and intentional with it; you have to do things that will build your skills. Most people choose to fill up their free time with easy, convenient, entertaining tasks such as social media. However, these things will not progress your life unless you work in the entertainment industry. Task stacking has the potential to give you extra hours in the day. Since I drive one hour each day and usually listen to podcasts, it's as if I added an extra hour to my day.

Maximize the value of your time by task stacking, making sure you have the materials on hand to do so. There is nothing worse for me than getting in the car without a podcast lined up. The default car behavior is turning on the radio, and that's not going to help me in the long run.

In short, task stacking will improve your productivity, and the wisdom acquired will give you an edge in society.

One of the best ways to experiment with your life is to become an early adopter. The following chart developed by Everette Rogers shows how society takes on a new idea or piece of technology.

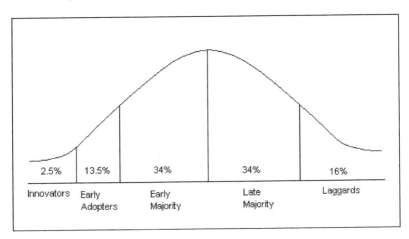

As you can see, there are innovators, early adopters, early majority, late majority, and laggards. Be an early adopter. Not everything you will do will become a success, but by being an early adopter, you give yourself more options and chances for a breakthrough.

I don't recommend trying to be an innovator because they tend to be taken over by the early adopters. Look at Facebook — it outgrew Myspace and Friendster and became a huge success. It's really hard to keep the lead as the innovator because there are many costs, and the first one to the market makes many mistakes. Early adopters can see what the innovators did and make improvements that will make their venture more successful. This is why you should read and learn from other's mistakes and successes. It will give you a better sense of which direction you should take in order to achieve your goals.

I strongly believe that podcasts are underrated tools for growth. To be an early adopter, you can't be afraid of losing money or time because that breakthrough moment will eventually come. However, you need to realize when it's time to jump ship and move on to the next thing. If you're an early adopter, you will be the lead person on a task that early and late majority adopters will still be wondering about. If you experiment, you will have the opportunity to pull from those experiences later in life. Being an early adopter means that you're a person of action. Don't let life pass you by. Have the courage to try something new and implement new ideas that you hear. Use your head and figure out what is best for you and discard the rest. To learn more about this topic, read *The Tipping Point* by Malcolm Gladwell.

Good things happen to those who hustle, and to hustle, you have to be the early adopter. Like everything else in life, being an early adopter takes effort and patience. It's just another useful tool you can use to make your life better. The early bird gets the worm, and the second bird gets whatever is left over.

To be an early adopter, you have to have information. You have to understand what is going on in your field and make conscious steps to become a master in that area. Knowledge will be the key to help you become that early adopter. Surround yourself with good mentors and influencers to see what is going on in your field. Find the area where you would like to be an early adopter and be so good that no one can ignore you. I like to stay on top of consumer technology, and I recommend that you follow Marques Brownlee. He is a master of being an early adopter, and he explains it in an informative yet enjoyable way. When I'm on the market for a new smartphone, I go directly to his YouTube page.

To be an effective early adopter, you must experiment with new ideas. I take certain ideas from podcasts and implement them into my business or life. If the ideas work and bring improvement, I keep them. If not, I discard them. Take a lesson from this book and see if it works for you. If it doesn't, drop it and try something else. If you're a laggard and never adopt anything new, you will expose yourself to the chopping block when life decides to change direction. Don't do that to yourself.

Meet New People

Meeting new people will set you apart. As Robert Greene says in *The 48 Laws of Power*, living in isolation is not a good idea. A fortress seems to be safe from the inside, but it cuts you off from valuable outside information and makes you an easy target. Don't stay isolated. Focus on meeting new groups of people so you gain new opportunities and know what's going on around you.

In one of my favorite books, *The Black Swan: The Impact of the Highly Improbable*, Nassim Taleb explains that low-probability events can hugely impact your life. These events can be thought of as "black swans." According to Taleb's example, every day for five years you see nothing but white swans, but one day you come across a black swan that changes the way you see the world. However, the only way you can see a black swan is if you're in a position to see it. This is why Taleb says it's important to get out and socialize. You don't know what insightful information you will hear or what offers you will receive.

A major black swan moment came for me when, while in the Marine Corps, I met my wife, Monica. It all happened because someone in my unit was busted for drug use. I happened to be in the same area as the Gunnery Sergeant in charge of sending people to Iraq when he announced that this Marine was getting kicked out and they needed someone to take his place. I wanted to go to Iraq, so I volunteered, and he selected me. I then began training to go to the sandbox, a.k.a. Iraq.

Before Marines go on an overseas deployment, they typically are allowed to take what's called pre-deployment leave, better known as time off. This allowed me a few weeks to see my family before spending months in the sandbox. I first visited my older sister in Chicago, and that's where I met Monica.

Meeting her changed my life completely, and I know it was for the better. If I hadn't met her, I doubt I would be living the great life I am now living because she helped strengthen a lot of my weaknesses. If I had stayed at home, I wouldn't be where I am today. Living in D.C. has made it even easier for me to take action to meet new people who will help challenge me and add value to my life.

Again, I highly recommend that you meet new people. You don't know what type of life you could be missing. People miss a lot of great opportunities by sitting on the sidelines and not taking action. When you interact with people, you have to be interesting and interested in others. This is why reading books and listening to podcasts can help. If you only watch television, you can only interact with people who watch the particular shows you watch. When I read books and listen to podcasts, I am able to accrue insightful information and have a dialogue with someone instead of a monologue. If you're socially awkward, I highly recommend listening to *The Art of Charm*. These podcasts will teach you how to become more charming, more interesting, and more confident. This takes practice, but you can make a difference if you work on it.

Never Eat Alone by Keith Ferrazzi is a book that will help you network in the 21st century. I was blown away by how helpful this book was. I loved Ferrazzi's story about how and why he networks. As you will see from Ferrazzi's stories, your network can determine your net worth. He describes specific examples of how he improved his network. One of his strategies to get to know people better and introduce them to each other is to host dinner parties. My wife and I also practice this.

I also like Ferrazzi's idea of hosting small parties with people who are influencers. This provides you with a chance to get to know them a little better and find ways you can provide value. I've hosted parties at which I've met new people and strengthened old relationships at the same time. Some people might say this is selfish, and if you do it in a malicious way, then yes, it is, but if you approach it from the perspective of "the whole is greater than the sum of its parts," you are actually doing a great thing. If you're doing something to create value and help other people, you're making the world a better place.

When it comes to meeting new people, don't come across as some-one only looking to push his own agenda. By meeting new people, you are ultimately doing something in your best interest, but your actions during the meeting should create a win-win scenario. One of my goals is to have a successful business, and I hope to use my business as a vehicle to create the change I want to see in the world. Another one of my goals is to cre-ate an endowment fund to enable Latinos to participate in professional internships in D.C. I love the Congressional Hispanic Caucus Institute (CHCI) that brought my wife to D.C. It provided her many opportunities that I was not aware of in Oregon, and I would like to pay it forward by giving others that same opportunity, but I need a solid network to make it happen.

When you're doing things for others that create a win-win sce-nario, you're working in society's best interest. This is the reason I love my job. I have the ability to help young Latinos and others pursue financial abundance. I share my experience and resources to improve their financial realities, and I am compensated for doing it. If I wasn't compensated, I wouldn't be able to pay my rent, pay my staff, or save toward my financial plan. It's a win-win situation because I intervene for people who would otherwise receive no attention. In my industry, the average financial advisor is white, male, and over 50 years old. This type of person is not routinely involved in the Latino community. I'm making a change in the world. If I didn't intervene with the Latino community, who would?

This motivates me to continue working on my craft. I devote 60 to 80 hours each week to grow my business. I am passionate about meeting Latinos and assisting them in their pursuit of their financial goals because I routinely see reports explaining that Latinos are not growing their wealth. I find that this is because no one helps them be intentional about their finances. I love coming into work because I know I'm making a difference. I'm excited about the future because I know I'm taking the right actions to become successful.

In order to reach more people, I follow five groups in the D.C. area that focus on Latino interests: LULAC, Prospanica, ALPFA, HBA-DC, and CHCI[4]. I dedicate my time to these groups by providing insight and making introductions. This connects me with other people that might need my services, and it gives me an outlet to demonstrate that I'm a trustworthy guy. It also helps people keep me in mind for the future.

If you're not involved, you will typically get ignored. Stay active. In my opinion, this is better than staying home alone. It's okay to do this occasionally, but put in the effort to sit down with people and have conversations that motivate all of you and help you grow professionally. Contribute to whatever group you're a part of and make sure you take action.

Follow-up is also important because hardly anyone does it. I usually like to follow up a conversation with an e-mail stating that it was great to meet that person. If I gained a piece of helpful advice, I explain how I used the information to make my life better. Follow-up is important if you want to be seen as a giver. I also recommend offering a LinkedIn request if you think you made a good connection. I post a lot of financial-planning-type material on my LinkedIn profile, and I want people to know that if you go with Joe, you can grow with Joe.

From John Corcoran's blog, *Smart Business Revolution*, I learned that we should try to make three introductions a day in which the people introduced will benefit from meeting each other. This will help us maintain

---

4   League of United Latin American Citizens, Association of Latino Professionals for America, Hispanic Bar Association – DC

and engage our weak-tie colleagues while also helping someone become a better version of himself. I strongly believe in giving a helping hand. Providing value to people makes them want to keep us around and gives opportunities to grow ourselves.

I'll say it once more — go out and meet new people. Hear their stories and find ways to make their lives easier. Don't worry about getting a one-to-one ratio of introducing to receiving. Focus on the inputs of giving and the outputs will eventually arrange themselves. It's like a lottery — you can only win if you pay for a ticket, so you have to accept that a few losses will come your way.

How to Improve Social Intelligence: Eventually You Have to Talk to Someone

Understanding people is crucial to success. You will constantly interact with other people, and how you interact with them will determine how successful you'll be. People like Charles Schwab and Andrew Carnegie were famous for how they interacted with people. If you want to be ultra-successful, you have to be able to influence people to do what you want them to do. This is why *How to Win Friends and Influence People* by Dale Carnegie is a must-read. There are so many great passages in the book; everyone should read it every one to two years. Two of the main principles in the book are smiling at people and calling them by their name. I love to practice these things in my day-to-day life.

By following the principles in this book, you can build relationships with people and understand how to give them value. From the gym and to the dry cleaner, I call people by their first names and chit chat with them, and they take care of me when I need it. If there is something I can do for them, I pay it forward. We create a win-win relationship that is worth the effort. I also ask people how they are doing. I especially like to ask if they are doing great. Some people are receptive, while others are not. I can't control their responses, but I can control mine.

Talking to people can also open opportunities. You never know who you are dealing with when you go out. Once when I was sitting in the airport, an older woman with a cup of ice cream sat down next to me. I smiled and said, "My name is Joe Bautista." She told me her name, and we started talking. I learned that her husband had been an NFL football player and currently worked for the NFL organization. I learned that she was a successful person herself — she sat on multiple boards for huge corporations. I received her business card, and now I know someone who works in this field. In the future, this could be helpful, or I may be able to introduce someone to her that could benefit someone else. This connection all started by telling her that her ice cream looked delicious and saying "Hi."

Don't expect that this trick will open the door for free stuff. Being a nice person and building relationships just shows that you care and that you're putting forth some effort. That's what it really comes down to — putting in effort. Energy is required in order for things to grow, so if you don't put in effort or take action, things won't grow and doors won't open. As with other things, you have to take action with relationships. Just make sure you're putting effort into the right relationships.

To make sure of this, read *Give and Take* by Adam Grant. In this book, Grant explains that there are four types of people — pushover givers, strategic givers, takers, and matchers. Pushover givers offer a lot of their time and resources to others and perform the worst in their jobs and relationships because they spread themselves too thin, burn out, and give opportunities to others. Strategic givers also offer a lot of their time and resources, but they perform the best in their jobs and relationships because they know how to avoid letting people take advantage of them while not giving up opportunities. A strategic giver can be duped by a taker, but usually only once.

Takers take advantage of givers who are pushovers and force an agenda without worrying about what happens to the givers. Matchers love to punish takers because they are more "quid pro quo" when it comes to giving and taking.

I am willing to give my time to others, but I know I have to be strategic. There are only 24 hours in each day, and I need to sleep during eight of those hours. You can make powerful connections with people if you have a giver mentality.

When you're just starting out in a business, you have to be a strategic giver. Find people worthy of your service and focus on helping them. I've come across people that are not worthy of being helped because they are takers. I've also come across many matchers and givers who provided me with great opportunities. Just focus on giving value to people, such as providing information in their industries, offering a connection, or simply listening to them. These actions will eventually pay off and give you more social capital.

As Jim Rohn said, "You are the average of the five people you spend the most time with." This is probably why Peter Voogd is passionate about hanging out with successful people. He says that if five of your friends are millionaires, you'll become the sixth, but if five of your closest friends are broke, you'll become the sixth one to go broke. I love surrounding myself with motivated people who are positive and want to get stuff done. I deal with a lot of stress through creating a business, and I need to surround myself with people who will help me achieve my goals and who want to grow themselves. Having the social intelligence to know who to surround yourself with will help you live a better life.

Active listening is also helpful for developing social intelligence. This is one area I have trouble with, but I'm working on it. I recommend "How to Keep the Conversation Going," episode 562 of *The Art of Charm*. We worked on this in *The Art of Charm* coaching sessions, and it was so helpful. I usually go on the question train when meeting people, and this doesn't really help us connect because those people feel like they are being interrogated. This is where active listening comes in: You hear what the person says and respond with something that builds rapport. In effect, you exchange stories instead of just basic facts (e.g., place of employment, hometown, or college degree). For example, someone you just met could say, "I have a dog," and you could reply, "I have a dog, too. He's a French bulldog named Kimo. What's your dog's name?" In this way you can build rapport. You can have deeper conversations with people and become more memorable if you master this skill.

Developing social intelligence has also helped me become a better husband. I'm not perfect, but I'm much better at communicating with my wife than I was a year ago. I was humble enough to admit that I struggled in this area, and I took action to improve by reading books like *The Feeling Good Handbook* by David D. Burns. Learning active listening and expressing my concerns in a constructive way were key to improving my marriage. Now we are even stronger as a couple. Having a strong marriage should be a priority; you can achieve this by listening to *The Art of Charm* toolbox, reading *How to Win Friends and Influence People*, and being intentional about implementing those ideas.

Bring High Value

I strongly believe in bringing value to your network, your workplace, and the world in general. This is how you make the pie bigger for society. You can bring value to a person by encouraging her to do more with her life, motivating her to do better, giving a recommendation that can help her in a certain aspect of her life, or complimenting her when she works to improve her craft or self.

We all know that game recognizes game. We should want people around us who improve us emotionally and physically while we do that for others in the process.

One way I try to bring value to people is by going through a circuit training workout with them. I love to work out with people because I see it as a win-win situation. We both get in a workout, we share an experience that we can pass on to others, and we have a chance to get to know each other better. Being "high value" basically means that you're positive and helpful in some way to those around you. Being negative and not participating or sharing are low-value characteristics. Low-value people bring energy levels down and do not allow others to accomplish nearly as much as they could.

I want to achieve more and help others do the same. I need to have the right people around me — high-value people. I was told by Johnny Dzubak, "The price of having low-value people in your life is your life."

Far too many people are not living the life they want to live because low-value people bring them down from what they want to accomplish.

Getting rid of low-value people can be a tough decision. If you're not strong enough to get rid of them or to tell them to change their lifestyles, they will continue to bring you down. It might be best to just start drifting in a new direction whether that means hanging out with a new group of people or finding a new job.

High-value people will help you achieve things you never thought you could achieve. My amazing wife, family, and friends motivate me to do great things, and I try to add value to them. To bring high value, you have to be in a good mood, be willing to do things for others, and be willing to experiment. Reclusiveness and negativity have no place in a high-value person.

Again, the body follows the mind and the mind follows the body. If you want results, you have to design your life to get results. A positive mindset will help you pursue that life. This is why I choose to put daily motivation and high-value people in my life. When I do so, my body and mind are in a pretty good spot.

Bringing high value also means putting in effort. It might seem difficult at first, but as you practice and seek feedback, you can determine how to bring high value. If someone replies with an enthusiastic "Thank you," you know you did a good job. Give high value to as many people as possible, but make sure it is for a good cause. Giving high value to a taker might not be a good idea if it drains too much of your time or resources. A quick five-minute favor is okay, but nothing more should be required unless you know it fits within your goals and lifestyle. Asking about someone's day or offering a smile takes little effort, but these are excellent ways to give value. Driving eight hours to deliver a passport to a good friend who forgot it is okay if he returns high value to you, but it is not okay if he is a low-value person taking advantage of you.

I work too hard in life to accept mediocrity. I'm glad I found a career that allows me to bring value to people and create a positive change in the world. Society would be better off with more high-value people. Do your part and be one of these people.

Make It Easy for People

One of the biggest life lessons I've learned is that you have to make it easy for people. Jordan Harbinger explains that most people try to give value the wrong way. He doesn't like when people ask, "How can I help you?" To give value to someone, offer a solution that will help. Spend time thinking how you can add value to that person. I like to use a CRM (customer relationship management) system to write down what people like and are passionate about. It's hard for me to remember everything, so I need a system. I like a CRM system because you can add reminders of important events and takeaways. Some people might say this is cheating, but adding information to your CRM takes work and effort on your part. *The Art of Charm* episode 294, called "Good Gift Giving: Why It's So Valuable," is all about how to make things easy for people. If you do this, they will be more likely to do what you want them to do.

If you want a letter of recommendation, simply write it for the person recommending you and have them make their own edits. You will be more likely to get it back faster while making the person's life easier. I saw this lesson during my time at the White House. There is so much work to be done that there is little time left for strategic thinking. This is why interns run the place. They do all the grunt work so the staff has time to work on big-picture ideas. This totally make sense because there are only 24 hours in each day, but America wants 96 hours of work done each day at the White House. In my current job, if I can make the process easy for people to follow, they are more likely to follow my recommendations.

However, making it easy for people requires you to gain skills and knowledge. I interact with people countless times each day, and if I can show them a shortcut on their phones or computers or show them how to use a piece of technology more efficiently, I have done my job to make their lives easier. Time is the scarcest resource, and people don't want to spend a lot of brain glucose to make decisions when they have other things to think about.

When you are handed a business card, write down important information on that card and follow up with an e-mail. I rarely receive follow-ups when I hand someone my business card. When you follow up with someone and remind them about a conversation you had, it shows that you care. By knowing this information about people, I am better able to know what they want. There are a lot of opportunities out there; you simply have to make it easy for people to give them to you.

If people put more effort into making things easy for others, the world would be a better place. If you have a boss, think of ways to help her out and make her look better. If you have an assistant, think of ways to make it easier for him to help you. I'm really good at using technology, so I take the time to help my assistant with computer issues because I know it will save me time down the road. In my career, we have to make sure that things don't slip through the cracks, or business will be lost. I give my clients quick fact sheets on steps they need to take to pursue their goals. There are many ways to make things easier for people, but you have to spend some time in thought.

By constantly learning, you will get new insight on how to provide value to people. If you ever have questions on how to do something, search YouTube. Many people won't look on YouTube to figure out their problems because they're too busy. It drives me crazy to see someone take thirty minutes to do something that could easily be done in ten minutes through a faster method. Gain skills and share those skills with others. If people know you can do many things, they are more likely to keep you around. Everyone wants to have helpful people around who can carry their own weight.

The Stronger Frame Will Dissolve the Smaller Frame

It's important to understand this concept because it will allow you to be more direct in pursuing your goals. For example, the book *Getting to Yes* by Bruce Patton, Roger Fisher, and William Ury explains that you can maintain a stronger frame in negotiation by remaining silent and waiting for the other person to speak after you ask a question or make an offer. This usually causes the other person to feel uncomfortable and allows you to get your way.

A strong frame will help you in your relationships, business, and life. Think back to a time when you were coerced into doing something because the other person had a stronger frame. Be firm in your beliefs. This doesn't mean you need to be overly aggressive and hostile. You can have a strong frame by having a strong positive attitude, which can dissolve a negative frame. Don't be around negative people all the time because their negative frames can chip away at the positive frame you're seeking. But when you are around negative people, smile and be friendly. You have the potential to turn a negative or neutral person into a positive person and give him a better day.

Believe that you're doing the right thing at the moment. You will constantly be challenged by opposing forces, and if your frame is weaker than your opponent's frame, you'll end up following that person. If someone is negative and your frame is already weak, you'll become negative. But if your frame is strong and positive, you can influence that person. If you can't, the best thing to do is move on. This is why I left my job at the Pentagon; I couldn't handle all the negativity. I'm glad I was able to see that I needed to leave and not be comfortable in staying. I could've ascended the ranks at the Pentagon, but it would've cost me my life.

I learned this way of living from Johnny Dzubak of *The Art of Charm*, and I wish I had learned the material sooner. It would've been helpful in so many situations. Since I can't change the past, I will just look for future opportunities to have that stronger frame so I can live the rest of my life the way I design it. I only have a set amount of time in this world, so I can't waste days or years on things I don't need in my life. This is why I need to maintain a strong frame and just live my life.

If you're dealing with a low-value person who has a stronger frame, you might have to walk away from the situation. As Benjamin Franklin said, "A man convinced against his will is of the same opinion still." Either find a different person to interact with or leave your current situation. Some things are not worth the time and energy, and you'll be less stressed out by saying "No" to the situation.

A strong frame for learning and executing will help you achieve your goals. If you let life keep you from achieving your goals, you have a weaker frame. Building a stronger frame requires repetition and energy. Compare this to blazing a trail through a forest. At first a lot of effort is required to clear the bushes, but after you walk the path enough times, it will become effortless and you won't have to think twice about maintaining that strong frame. To reach your goals, you have to work through the challenge of making a path. A strong frame prevents you from quitting the process, and knowing your "why" will give you the reason to build that strong frame.

In *The Alchemist* by Paulo Coelho, you'll learn that the path less traveled usually holds treasure at the end. Things that can be easily obtained are usually not good for you. Television, video games, and social media are easy activities, but they don't offer much growth. The hard things in life, like going to bed and waking up early, reading professional development books, exercising, and meeting new people, will make you a better person and give you a stronger frame. As Charlie Munger said, "The world is not yet a crazy enough place to reward a whole bunch of undeserving people." You have to work on creating your path. If you're doing something uncomfortable, that usually means you're clearing your path. Work on your frame by doing things that are uncomfortable, and have positive energy. I'm constantly working on my strong frame, and I will achieve my goals because of it.

The Victim Mindset vs. The Achievement Mindset

The hosts of *The Art of Charm* talk a lot about the victim mentality. If you tell yourself that things are too tough or that you don't deserve a certain outcome, you're playing the victim card. Understanding emotional intelligence and emotional healing will help you overcome a victim mentality. For more advice, listen to episodes 327 and 328 of *The Art of Charm.*

One way to have a victim mentality is to apologize for things that are out of your control or believe that things are set in stone. When you play the victim, you won't achieve the things you desire in life. This can bring regret and lower your self-esteem. Not everything will go smoothly, but you have to view negative experiences as obstacles to overcome, not as stop signs. Self-defeating talk is also a bad habit because it affects your self-esteem. To deal with life, you need an achievement mindset.

I'm so happy with how my life is turning out. I set my goals, then I put effort into achieving those goals. If something goes wrong in the process, I look for more knowledge and another strategy to move forward. To understand why an achievement mindset is important, read *Learned Optimism* by Martin Seligman and *Emotional First Aid* by Guy Winch.

If you play the victim, you're waiting to be saved because you're not strong enough to handle the situation. When a problem arises, it is important to know that you can outgrow the problem and invent a solution to overcome it because the problem doesn't own you. It's just temporary. Be consistent about not playing the victim card, and be aware of yourself. Ask your family or friends if they think you complain too much. If you do, change your attitude. If you find yourself wanting to do something but find an excuse not to do it, come up with a plan to achieve it or change what you want in life. There is no time to play the victim.

Some people play the victim because of fear, and fear's best friend is rationalization, as Steven Pressfield said in *The War of Art: Break Through the Blocks and Win Your Inner Creative Battles*. It's easy to rationalize why you can't do something because you're afraid of the outcome or think you can't do it. The best way to handle fear is to just deal with it and realize that you can bounce back from it. It will feel awkward and sometimes painful, but when you do something enough times, it becomes second nature. Don't let rationalization hold you back. Go after what you want by having that achievement mindset, and eventually things will go your way. If one opportunity doesn't go well, convince yourself that it's fine because another one will come your way, just like a bus at a bus stop.

The sales funnel is a good example of an achievement mindset. In sales, you will face a lot of rejection, but keep pushing through and know that you can make it. If you play the victim, you will see the rejection as your fault or someone else's fault, and you won't continue. The achievement mindset is crucial because it allows you to brush off those rejections and focus on someone who needs you. If enough opportunities are in front of you, you will eventually reach your goals. We live in a world full of opportunities; you just need the right mindset.

The same thing can happen with dating; you have to kiss a lot of frogs to find your prince. If things are not going well, analyze the situation and see what you need to do for better results. If you *want* more in life, you have to *be* more. With the achievement mindset, you realize that you can work on yourself to become better and have the relationships you deserve.

I love setting goals and challenging myself to improve. When I set a goal and achieve it, I feel amazing, but I know I have to set a new goal. To have the achievement mindset, you must have persistence and the willingness to learn. I am very coachable, and this helps me become a better person; if someone tells me to do something and I trust her judgement, I usually do it, and it turns out well for me.

If someone with the victim mindset tells me not to do something or that I can't do it, I usually just ignore him, avoid him, and continue to work on my goals. As Arnold Schwarzenegger said, "I love it when someone says that no one has ever done this before because then, when I do it, that means that I'm the first one that has done it." The achievement mindset helps you do the unthinkable and create an abundant lifestyle. The victim mindset will never allow you to accomplish anything great, and we need to do great things to move the world forward. We can't afford the luxury of allowing things to stay the same because the world will change whether we like it or not. The achievement mindset will put you on a different level by allowing you to deal with change. Since you're changing and growing as a person, you can handle the changes of life. It is crazy how good I feel because I'm working on things I want to work on versus slaving to the dictates of life. This is why I love living in the United States. Here I have the opportunity to work on myself, grow myself, and help others achieve their goals.

Sometimes, though, you have to endure obstacles to live a better life. I joined the military because I wanted to receive free education. I applied to the University of Oregon and Gonzaga and was accepted to both. I saw the tuition bill and thought, "I need to get this paid for" because the only other way was student loans. So I joined the Marines. I didn't play the victim and complain that it was unfair that I had to go into the military to pay for college. I just looked at my situation and saw that the military could help me achieve my goals. The military pays for schooling for a reason; I experienced some of the worst days of my life in the military due to the lack of control. I didn't have the right mindset, and it really affected me, but joining the military was a good move overall. Now when people complain about their student loans, I just think to myself, "I'm glad that's not an issue I have to deal with." Sometimes you have to do things you don't want to do in order to achieve your goals.

Now that I have the achievement mindset, I don't see inconveniences as burdensome. I just see them as something I have to overcome to reach my goals. To deal with the inconveniences of life, write down your goals. Review them to make sure you are staying on track with the achievement mindset. It is always wise to focus on the small wins. Even if you don't get the business deal or the date, you receive a small win knowing you took action to move yourself toward your goal; you simply found out that the option wasn't worth taking. Edison needed thousands of tries to finally produce the light bulb, and instead of viewing those as failures, he reasoned that he had simply found a thousand different methods that didn't work. He knew how to take small victories in the right direction.

I recommend that you record in your journal a small victory you accomplish each day. This will help train your mind for achievement. If you are aware of what you are doing and focus on it, you will improve. An achievement mindset is crucial if you want to be successful in this world and do great things.

You Have to Be Hungry

A great YouTube video that I watch on a weekly basis is *Are You Hungry* by Les Brown. It is so motivating, and I love listening to it while I'm getting ready in the morning. It represents everything I need to do in my life. Les Brown has come up with a lot of great one-liners and has a passionate voice. In this video, he describes the need to push through the hard times and take control of your life. He explains that you are the writer of your life's script, the film director, and the producer. You will determine if your "film" will be a box office hit or a flop. When I'm feeling unmotivated, this nine-minute video tells me everything I need to do to make my dream work.

I'm so hungry to achieve my goals. I want to be a successful financial advisor, helping people build their financial wealth so they can live abundantly. I also want to create an endowment fund to help other Latinos achieve opportunities they might not otherwise have. These motivational speeches have changed my life and help me stay hungry as I focus on my goals.

I'm all about improving myself and helping others. To do this, though, I have to be hungry and relentless about achieving my goals. If it takes many years to do this, that's okay because I know I'm doing what I'm supposed to be doing. As long as I'm hungry and putting in the effort, I'm okay with the process. The journey is the best part of your life; it's where you get your stories. Take time to reminisce about what you did to get where you are now. People want to hear a story, not facts, and you need to be prepared to show vulnerability and put it out there.

Being relentless and hungry will help you pursue your goals and get more out of life. If I wasn't hungry, I wouldn't have accomplished as much as I have in my life. I feel like I haven't wasted much time in the last five years because I've been constantly working on my goals, and when you're hungry and you hustle, your goals become clearer and you can identify what type of person you are or want to become.

Les Brown's motivational speeches are amazing, and I recommend that you start listening to this particular video on a regular basis. I like to listen to it and review my goals so I know what I'm working toward and why my goals are worthwhile. Life is a roller coaster, and videos like this will help you deal with the rough times.

The Fortune is in the Follow-up

As a financial advisor, I conduct a lot of follow-up with people. This is crucial. If you search "The Fortune is in the Follow-Up!" through Google, you will see an intriguing photo stating the following:

- 48 percent of people never follow up with a new prospect
- 25 percent make a second contact and stop
- 12 percent make a third contact and stop
- Only 10 percent make more than three contacts
- 2 percent of sales are made on the first contact
- 3 percent of sales are made on the second contact
- 5 percent of sales are made on the third contact
- 10 percent of sales are made on the fourth contact
- 80 percent of sales are made on the fifth to twelfth contacts

There is a fortune to be made from actually following up with people. When I was in the Marine Corps, follow-up was key to success. Countless times, tasks weren't accomplished because proper follow-up wasn't conducted. I was in charge of spending and keeping track of the budget for my battalion, and we had special training funds. When exercises were being performed that required many moving parts, following up with different sections to monitor progress gave me an idea of what needed to happen. I had to make sure people were doing what they were supposed to be doing, and taking five minutes to do a progress report saved a lot of headache. If I had not followed up, the equipment would not have been ordered, there would have been no training exercise, and we would have endured long days because everyone has to pay the price in the Marines.

Some great tools for follow-up are Google Voice, Google Keep, Evernote, and Microsoft Outlook. If I'm at work, Evernote and Microsoft Outlook work the best. Since my job is very dependent on e-mail and phone calls, Microsoft Outlook has been amazing. I can connect tasks to my calendar and e-mails by simply hitting the follow-up button and selecting the day and time I need to follow up. This is incredible because when I'm dealing with other people's files, it's hard to keep track of everything in my brain.

To make sure I'm covering all my important tasks, I like to review them in the morning before I start my day. I also check to see if I need to postpone anything to another day. When I need to call someone, I make sure to put notes about that person in front of me to help me remember what to talk about. I also make notes about things that are important to the person. If you're in a relationship-based service, it's important to actively listen and write down important details, such as a client's vacation or his child's competition, so you can discuss it the next time you meet. If a client tells you his favorite band and favorite type of food and you let him know when that band is coming to town and that there is a new restaurant in town that he might like, he will be grateful. In addition, he will know that you care and that you are putting effort into the relationship.

By following these principles, you will help people remember you and think of you when opportunities arise. Stay in contact with people you know and introduce yourself to new people. If you see someone outside of your regular meetings, be sure to show high energy and have a smile on your face. Follow-up is all about receiving and sending opportunities. This is how we grow the social opportunities pie. You may not always have time to do a thorough follow-up, but a spot check is fine most of the time.

Follow-up is all about effort and being intentional. It is best to have a system in place to help you accomplish your follow-up mission. I love using Google Now to help me with reminders. When I go to the dry cleaner, I usually tell my smartwatch to remind me to pick up my clothes at the right time. More often than not, if something isn't written down, it doesn't happen. Writing down your goals and reviewing them once a week is crucial so that you know which direction you are headed and don't drift too far from your path.

People lead busy lives and need reminders. If you are a new business owner starting without an assistant, one of the biggest things you can do is confirm your appointments through phone calls and e-mails. If you are nervous about trying phone calls, don't think people don't like you. If someone did not specifically say "No" to you when you tried to call them, keep trying. When a phone call or e-mail goes unanswered, imagine that the recipient was extremely busy and couldn't communicate with you at the time you reached out. This very thing happens to me. Sometimes, even though I have every intention of returning someone's message, I forget to reply because I get distracted. Keep following up.

In business, it really can take up to 12 contacts to finally reach a person and get that meeting. Don't take a lack of response personally because it is something you can't control, and it can make the phone feel like it weighs 700 pounds. This is all a mental problem; take action to get over it. Reassure yourself that people need the service you provide. As Grant Cardone wrote in *Sell to Survive*, you have to believe in your product and buy it. You have to have 100 percent buy-in to make it happen. People can tell if you are not serious about your product and will feel skeptical to buy it from you.

Finally, don't be dependent on outcome; don't put all your hope into one deal because the sure thing is not a sure thing. Focus on the inputs because you can't control outcomes when other people are involved. When you depend on the outcome, you will feel devastated when it doesn't come true. In my organization, we constantly preach against being outcome dependent. Try not to lose that mindset when things are not going your way.

Not being outcome dependent will make that phone feel a lot lighter. Be in constant communication with people so they remember why they need to do business with you. Constantly fill your sales funnel. Create a follow-up system and wait for the opportunities to come to you because you did the work of following up.

Possible but Not Probable

One of my biggest pet peeves is the lottery. It's possible to win it all, but it's also very unlikely. Too many people try to take the easy way out to overcome their problems. I find that the biggest keys to success are discipline and hard work. Most successes do not come overnight but from long-term dedication. It may not be very popular to go to the gym every day and eat properly while others drink beer and watch television, but if your goal is to lose weight or be healthy, you have to be willing to do what is uncomfortable.

If you want more, you have to be more. This means you need more skills and must become so good at your craft that you can't be ignored. It's possible to have a great life with little skills, but it's not very probable. I love my life because it's a journey of constant growth. I can control how much time I spend reading books, how many people I talk to and make new connections with, how little television I watch, and how much time I dedicate to my craft. Life is a balance, and you must determine what you need to do to obtain the life you want.

The Art of Charm makes an interesting suggestion: Don't visualize having a big home or fancy car. Instead, visualize the steps it will take to get those things. When you imagine the car or home, you tell your mind that you already have those things. This causes a lack of motivation. Focus on the process that can lead to your desired outcome.

No matter what goal you want to accomplish, focus on the process. Don't worry about making a big difference right away. Worry about the things you need to do on a daily basis. Personally, I need to make many phone calls and send out e-mails to people in order to bring them on as clients. For me, an increase in phone calls and e-mails will improve my probability of success. Larry Bird shot 500 free throws each day to work on his craft. How many "free throws" are you practicing on a daily basis? It's possible to make three free throws in a row, but how consistent will you be if you don't practice your skills? You are much more likely to be consistent when you practice. It will take time and there will be setbacks, but practice will prepare you for these disadvantages.

If you're just starting out, don't forget to hedge your activities. In the book *Originals* by Adam Grant, the most successful clients had an income to fall back on in case things didn't go right. When I was applying to college, I was worried about taking on a lot of school loan debt. When I received my acceptance letter from Gonzaga University and saw how much tuition would cost, I thought, "I'm going to the military to pay for this." As I've already attested, it was one of the best moves I've made because it gave me so much flexibility down the line. Because the G.I. Bill paid for my tuition and gave me a monthly allowance for housing, I was able to quit my job and go back to school to study economics. I maximized my education by obtaining two bachelor's degrees and will soon have an MBA with no student loan debt.

If you come across opportunities to improve yourself, take advantage. It is very unlikely that you will be able to make a difference without gaining new skills or experience. It's the reason I'm always going to school, even while working. I'm willing to do both because I need to accomplish a lot in my life. Life is about gaining experience and being disciplined. The harder you work, the more luck you will have.

In a sporting event, the one who hustles has more opportunities to score. This is also true in life. The more you hustle and grind, the more you will come across opportunities. I don't expect life to give me anything; I have to work and put in effort. I have to make connections and provide value to people. The more I do this, the more likely I am to achieve my goals. This is why I read 36 books each year, listen to 20 hours of podcasts each week, and watch motivational or educational YouTube videos.

I love that I'm able to learn new skills and apply them to others. This is how society grows. In one of my public health classes, my professor, Deb Harris, told me that you can't save the whole world, but you can save a piece of it. This is exactly what I focus on.

Personally, I focus on helping Latinos build their wealth. I can accomplish this goal because I'm a master in the language of money. There is a big minority gap in the field of financial services, and I want to be the change that makes a difference in that field. Accomplishing this dream will take hard work, but I see it as probable because I'm putting the energy into growing myself and expanding my possibilities.

Don't put your faith in low-probability events. Make your own luck through action and persistence because the best way to predict the future is to create it.

Be Mindful of the Present

I know I've talked a lot about working hard and never quitting. You certainly have to do these things, but it is also important to be mindful of the present. Take time out of your day to shut down and relax. You will burn out if you're constantly going at 100 miles per hour. I still take time out of each day to talk to people and partake in social media, but I limit that time. I don't really like watching television, but if that's what you want to do, it's fine in moderation.

Like I said, the stories come from the journey, not the destination, so be conscious of what is happening in the present. Write down your thoughts and things you're grateful for in a journal. This will serve as a barometer for how your life is going. I let some things that were important to me get too far from me, and I paid the price in terms of my relationship with my wife. Because I was focused on the future, I didn't realize that what I thought was important was not very important in the first place. I'm glad I was able to recognize my errors, and I'm taking steps to fix them. I learned a very valuable lesson, and I won't disregard the present anymore. Now that I try to be mindful of the present, I feel much more calm and satisfied with life. I still try to do what is important for my future goals, but it only makes up a portion of my day.

As Tai Lopez says, you have to optimize your day. If you go on a vacation, optimize the vacation. If you're focusing on things outside the vacation and not enjoying the scenery, it won't be a very good vacation. On a great vacation, you enjoy the moment and have time to reflect on how good the present is.

When it comes to important relationships, you have to invest in them to make them grow. Like I said, time and decay move in the same direction, and if you don't put any energy into your relationships, they won't grow. Optimize each day in terms of your career, relationships, body, wealth, and mind. Most of the time, I can't accomplish everything I want to do in a day, and most major things in life take time to accomplish. So don't worry too much about not completing everything at once.

In each day, you can really only work four hours on the important stuff. In the book *Deep Work*, Newport says that we can usually only focus on something for those four hours before we start to see diminishing returns on our time. Don't try to do something with 50 percent energy. Do each task with 100 percent energy and focus on a different task when you start to slow down. Sometimes you need to do less work instead of more work. A well-placed break can give you time to recharge, be more creative, and release stress. Diminishing returns is a real thing, and when you go too hard and too fast, eventually, although you press the gas pedal, your life will just slowly move forward or not at all because you ran out of gas.

We have to focus on many things, and it can be very overwhelming. This is why taking breaks is important. Breaks provide opportunities to reset your brain and become more efficient. It's kind of like sharpening an axe. If you never take the time to perform this task, the axe will become more and more dull with every swing and eventually won't be able to cut down a tree.

One great way to clear your mind is to meditate. Reading a book like *10% Happier: How I Tamed the Voice in My Head, Reduced Stress Without Losing My Edge, and Found Self-Help That Actually Works—A True Story* by Dan Harris would be a good start to learn the importance and practice of meditation. I currently meditate in the sauna after I work out in the gym.

I just close my eyes and focus on breathing. It's okay if your mind wanders because you need to train your brain like a muscle. When you realize your mind has wandered, discard it and focus again on your breathing. I like to imagine my breath traveling from my mouth to one section of my body. I start by taking a deep breath and focusing my breath to my feet, then I slowly release my breath. With the next breath, I focus my breath to my ankles. I keep following the process until I reach the top of my head, and then I start over again. This helps me focus on my day. If, during the day, I noticed I'm feeling stressed out, I take 30 seconds to just focus on my breathing. This allows me to reset my brain. A lot of the podcasts I listen to praise the benefits of meditating. I think the biggest benefit is the removal of stress. Chronic stress is very toxic to our systems, and we need to develop a process for removing it from our bodies. Meditating only takes 5–10 minutes, but it is probably one of the most productive 5–10 minutes of my day.

Saying "No" to things is also important to help you stay focused on the present. James Altucher stresses this concept. By saying "No," we can free ourselves from thinking about things we don't really want to do. Understand what is important to you and make those things your priorities. When you say "Yes" to one thing, you're saying "No" to another, and vice versa. Only say "Yes" to things that are really important to you because your time is very valuable and can never be replenished. Saying "Yes" means you're giving up your present for someone else's present. So saying "No" is an important concept because it will free up a lot of time for yourself if you do it correctly. *On The Shortness of Life* by Seneca is another important read on the power of "No" because life can stretch really long if you know how to use it correctly. Over 2000 years ago, Seneca knew the importance of saying "No":

> *"People are frugal in guarding their personal property; but as soon as it comes to squandering time they are most wasteful of the one thing in which it is right to be stingy."*

Time is more valuable than property, but most people mix these up. This is why optimizing your time based on your goals is so important. I need to make sure I'm prioritizing my day — taking care of the important stuff like making sure my wife feels loved and building myself professionally. You can always make another dollar, but you can't make another hour. Being present in the moment is very hard to do because we see that other people have what we want out of life, and react by not being grateful for where we stand. Be patient with life. If you do the right things, the things you want will eventually come, but enjoy the present as it is happening. If the things I want out of life don't come my way, I'm okay with it. If I died tomorrow, I would be fine because I optimized my life to the best of my ability. I'm not perfect and no one is, but I know I live life on my terms by staying focused on the future while living in the present.

Conclusion

To be successful in life, follow Tai Lopez's K.S.E. model — knowledge, strategy, and execution. This is exactly the type of process that will help you grow yourself as a person.

First, if you want to be a better person in a particular area, you must have sufficient knowledge about that area. When I was a kid and played Madden™ on my PS2™, I would read the manual to learn how to do certain moves. When I played against someone who hadn't read the manual, I usually beat that person because I had the knowledge to beat him. When I have knowledge and my opponent doesn't, I usually win.

This is where reading, listening to podcasts, and watching YouTube videos comes in. These tools increase your knowledge, improve your life, and give you a better shot at outperforming your competition. Here is the clincher: The person you should be competing against is yourself. This month's version of yourself should able to beat last month's version because of the new skills and experiences you have accumulated in that time. Each day, make sure to brush up on your skills and go to bed a little wiser than when you woke up. This incremental progress in knowledge will make a difference in the long run. Knowledge is the foundation because the more you learn, the more you earn.

Second, you need strategies to help you reach your goals. When you're trying to accomplish something, have a general idea of what you need to do. Strategies are concepts and rules that help you achieve your goal. They should be flexible and comprehensive because there is a lot of uncertainty in the world and things will go wrong. As Mike Tyson once said, "Everyone has a plan 'till they get punched in the mouth." Understanding what could go wrong and having a solid strategy will save you time and give you more opportunities for success. Seeking information from external sources will help you formulate a good strategy for pursuing your goals. It is also a good idea to evaluate your plans so you can learn from past mistakes and miscues.

Finally, you need to execute; it is the most important step to take. Many people don't execute. They just sit and wait for things to come to them. But I'm a firm believer in this saying by Abraham Lincoln: "Things may come to those who wait, but only the things left by those who hustled." Execute the things you learn from all the books, podcasts, and YouTube videos you will be consuming. There is so much advice available, and it will be difficult to know which path to follow, but I recommend you watch the most successful people and mimic them. They write books and make podcasts and YouTube videos because they want that information to be used, and they want to be credited for it. If you use someone's knowledge or strategy, make sure you send them a kind note to let them know they helped you. You may not be able to help them, but you can make them feel good by letting them know they helped you become a better person.

Then, to go from good to great, start incorporating the deep work mindset. Focus on becoming the best person you can be by seeking your goals with a strategy and plan in place. Most people think they can reach success with one social media or blog post, but it usually takes seven to ten years of work to become a success. It is incremental execution that differentiates the average from the great.

Reading *Deep Work* is a beneficial first step to becoming great. Discipline is a trait that successful people share in common. Saying "No" to something unimportant is difficult, and it requires you to be uncomfortable. That unimportant thing might be fun now, but it won't get you anywhere in the future. If you can't do something at work because of all the distractions, try to do it at home in an isolated area.

I think it is also crucial to set up time to exercise. As I said earlier, the mind follows the body and the body follows the mind. If you're in shape, you'll have more confidence and energy. Reading is also key because the more we know, the more we grow. Since we only have one life, we shouldn't live in mediocrity. That is why it's necessary to execute on these important tasks like exercising and reading. I haven't lived a perfect life, but I feel like, because of execution, I have made a bigger dent than others in solving my life's math problem.

Entrepreneur Peter Voogd is big on execution. In an interview with *Addicted 2 Success*, Peter said that only five percent of people who watch or read personal development content actually implement it. This fact blew my mind, but I can see how it is true. Taking lessons from other people and applying them to your life can be difficult, and the obstacles that come up can put you off course. Taking action is what sets people apart, but it has to be constant action. You will probably have to try something 100 times before you succeed and reach your ultimate goal. If you don't know what to do, just do something, but don't be married to that thing because you might have to change your game plan.

The best way to execute is to break things down into simple steps. You can't eat an elephant in one bite, but you can finish eating that elephant one bite at a time, over a long period. To write this book, I compiled examples of lessons that I learned and enjoyed. I didn't seek to write a 200-page book in one sitting. I just took in one topic at a time and set a goal of writing four pages each week. At first I wrote two pages each week, but as soon as I reached 20 pages, four pages was much more exciting because I felt like I was going to finish in half the time.

If you need to start exercising, for example, make the process as simple as possible. Have your gym clothes and lunch ready the night before so that all you have to do in the morning is get your body to the gym. I often tell people, "You don't have to be great to get started. You just have to get started to become great." So don't think about the task; just execute on it. Again, don't try to eat the whole elephant at one time. I usually try to work out and practice my Spanish at least five times a week. I don't shoot for this weekly goal. I just take it one day at a time. I look at each day and schedule when I can go to the gym. By prioritizing, I am more success-ful because I am forced to be accountable to myself. Take small steps and build your momentum by optimizing the day. It is less stressful to only think on one day's worth of tasks instead of a month's worth.

Don't say, "Tomorrow or next year I will start" because you'll very likely be the same person with the same excuses later. If you need motiva-tion, listen to Peter Voogd, Eric Thomas, and Les Brown. Many of us have dreams of better lives, but the distance between a dream and reality is ac-tion or execution. There are no other paths. Your dream will not be given to you unless you work for it.

My dad works hard to get things done. He knows how to execute what he is great at. I have his same work ethic, and I want to pay him back one day. My dad wanted a better life than the one he had in Oaxaca, Mexico. Things were rough, and he decided to move to the United States to have a better life. He achieved his dream. He went through a lot of obstacles and tough times by working in the fields as an immigrant and getting deported back to Mexico a couple of times, but he made it to a better place through hard work and by treating others well.

Action, action, action will take us to the next level. So many people want to wait for that fresh start. They want to wait until next month or next year or after a certain event because they don't feel like beginning. Like AJ Harbinger said "It's better to act to feel than to feel to act", mean-ing that the motivation to start something will come from the action you take first and not waiting until you feel like doing something. For me, the motivation to work toward my goals does not happen because I *feel* moti-vated. It usually comes when I take action and see progress. By waiting to take action when you feel like it, you force yourself to climb a steeper and steeper hill. As Warren Buffett said, "The chains of habit are too weak to be felt until they are too heavy to be moved." I strongly believe that how you do anything is how you do everything. Set a standard that you want other people to follow.

Make sure you write down the lessons you learn and apply them to your life. Many people tell us what to do, but many of those same people don't do what is necessary to change their lives. If you fail at something, follow up with another attempt because the fortune is in the follow-up. Eventually the persistence and dedication will pay off.

For example, as I have said many times, I want to become the best financial advisor by becoming so good that I can't be ignored. To do this, I dedicate a lot of time to crafting my skills and building my reputation. I don't watch television and I rarely watch sports. I want the good life in which I have control over what I do, and I need to become a business owner to do that. I also want to help people pursue their financial goals and ensure they have the best strategies in place. I am just starting off in my career, but I am a better financial advisor than I was six months ago, and I will be even better six months from the time you're reading this sentence. This is because I am constantly working to better my craft. To do this, I have to execute — do what it takes to become better. It can be boring sometimes, but I need to do it to become successful.

Along with reading books, listening to podcasts, and watching YouTube videos, seek a coach and receive mentoring. I plan to do this in my own journey of ultimate progress. As seen in many biographies, all successful people had someone to help them achieve the best version of themselves. Talk to the people you want to emulate, and hire a coach or mentor to bring it all together. Go out there and learn from all the sources you can. If you don't, you will just be average and will be left behind. You should want a great life; make it worthwhile by being good, gaining knowledge and strategies, and executing.

To start, I recommend you write down some goals you would like to achieve in the future. Then focus your time and energy on achieving those goals by being intentional, not casual. Exciting things typically do not happen to people who are casual and comfortable. Go out and get what you are after. Read one motivating book and one book to improve your skills. Do a Google search to find podcasts to improve your life. Find YouTube videos for motivation and to help you with certain skills.

A great resource to help you figure out what type of person you are and what you should be doing is 5 Dynamics. I'm a workaholic, and this is one reason I like being in D.C. There is so much to do here, and I'm never bored. Taking a personality test really helped me understand the person I am and pointed out my weaknesses and strengths.

Becoming the best version of yourself will take time. I have only been serious about reading books and listening to podcasts for about four years now. I wish that time was longer, but we don't start out as great people. It might take you one year or ten years to become the successful person you want to be, but it can only happen if you try and stick with it. I'm a much better person now than I was in the past, and this same progress can happen in your life.

I would like others to benefit in the same ways I have. (This is one reason I wrote this book.) I'm always offering knowledge to my friends by sharing new insights I learn and helpful passages I've read. As I've mentioned, my goal is to read 1000 books before I die, and I will read at least 36 books each year until I achieve that goal. I'm about 20 to 25 years from reaching that milestone, and I expect to reap a lot of value in that time. This value will enable me to leverage the knowledge I receive, be successful in my career, and gain more control over my life. It will also help me be more creative in my job. I give advice for a living, and I need to make sure that my advice is of the highest quality I can provide. Since most of this information will become obsolete in the future, I have to continue to increase my knowledge and never stop being a student. I used to have fantasies of retiring and playing video games all day, but that is not the case anymore. I'm going to be active for a long time, and I will continue to be so good that I can't be ignored.

I believe feedback is important, and it's the reason I started a book club that focuses on reading personal growth books. The book club provides feedback on how a book did or did not improve the lives of the readers, and I can learn from this feedback. If you love personal growth as much as I do, I highly recommend that you start a book club, as well. It only has to include five participants. Remember that you are the average of the five people you spend the most time with, so hang out with people who will push you to become better, who will improve you, and whom you can improve. Steel sharpens steel.

I hope you enjoyed this book. Feel free to share this experience with others. Your life goal should be to make each year your best year ever, and I hope this book will lead you down that path.

Closing Remarks

I do all that I do because I can't be satisfied with mediocrity. I have to be great because I didn't grow up with the same socioeconomic standards of other members of my community, and I knew I could grow myself into the standard of living I wanted.

I grew up in a mobile home with two parents who worked extremely hard to give me opportunities in my life. My dad worked Monday to Monday without complaint about the long hours. He has an uncanny work ethic that he passed on to me. He was deported back to Mexico five times, but he came back six. Why would I waste any opportunities here in the United States when my dad tried so hard to stay here? Thank God he worked hard, allowing me to be here now. I feel like I would be slapping my dad in the face if didn't give 110 percent and accomplish something great. My dad made it to where he is now because of hard work. I will follow his path because I know it works.

I couldn't stand working in the Marines or the Federal Government because some people were not willing to put in as much effort as I was. I can't control other people, but I can control what I do. All I want to do is accomplish the change I want to see in the world. I want to be one of the greatest financial advisors, and this will require a lot of work. If I'm not the best, I'm heading toward it. I will reach my goal, and I'm willing to take any measures to get there. Ultimately, I want to help as many Latinos as possible achieve financial abundance and prevent them from suffering financially. This is my life meaning, and I love it. If I want extraordinary results, I must do what others are not willing to do.

Don't be one of many people who waste their potential. Know what you want out of life and pursue it. Have a purpose, a plan, and a drive, and, as Tim Grover says, you will move from good to great to unstoppable.

Top 15 Books

- *The Subtle Art of Not Giving a Fuck: A Counterintuitive Approach to Living a Good Life* by Mark Manson
- *The 50th Law* by 50 Cent and Robert Greene
- *Give and Take: A Revolutionary Approach to Success* by Adam Grant
- *Start with Why: How Great Leaders Inspire Everyone to Take Action* by Simon Sinek
- *The Obstacle Is the Way: The Timeless Art of Turning Trials into Triumph* by Ryan Holiday
- *Good to Great: Why Some Companies Make the Leap . . . and Others Don't* by James Collins
- *So Good They Can't Ignore You: Why Skills Trump Passion in the Quest for Work You Love* by Cal Newport
- *Outliers: The Story of Success* by Malcolm Gladwell
- *Who Moved My Cheese?* By Spencer Johnson
- *Nudge: Improving Decisions about Health, Wealth, and Happiness* by Richard Thaler
- *Never Eat Alone: And Other Secrets to Success, One Relationship at a Time* by Keith Ferrazzi
- *Sell to Survive* by Grant Cardone
- *Meditations* by Marcus Aurelius
- *The 48 Laws of Power* by Robert Greene
- *The Black Swan: The Impact of the Highly Improbable* by Nassim Nicholas Taleb

Top 15 YouTube Videos
(To find these videos on YouTube, just type the title into the search bar.)

- "Best Motivational Speech Compilation Ever #2 — 30-Minute Motivation #2"
- "Best Motivational Speech — Watch This to Start Your Day, EveryDay!!"
- "Arnold Schwarzenegger Motivation — 6 Rules of Success Speech – with subtitles [HD]"
- "The Light at the End of the Tunnel | Motivational Video"
- "Les Brown — It's Possible"
- "Les Brown: I AM Going to Make It . . ."
- "Oprah Winfrey's Top 10 Rules for Success (@Oprah)"
- "Steve Harvey on Life — Wow! Great Advice . . ."
- "It's Not OVER Until You Win! Your Dream is Possible — Les Brown"
- "Jim Rohn's | Top 10 Rules for Success"
- "Eric Thomas's Top 10 Rules for Success"
- "Make a Decision — Motivational Video"
- "DO WHAT IS HARD — Motivational Video"
- " 'Are You Hungry?' Motivational Workout Speech"
- "MM 12 DISCIPLINE: No More Excuses [HD] Ft. Eric Thomas, Jeffery Moore, and Les Brown"

Top 15 Podcasts:

- The James Altucher Show, "Ep. 181: Jordan Harbinger — The Mindset We All Want"
- The James Altucher Show, "Ep. 157 — Gary Vanyerchuk: Be Successful By Being Yourself"
- The James Altucher Show, "AA Ep. 339 — Cassey Ho: YouTube's Biggest Fitness Instructor, Tells How She Did It Her Way"
- The James Altucher Show, "Ep. 133 — Tucker Max: Mate: Become the Man Women Want"
- The James Altucher Show, "Ep. 115 — Freeway Rick Ross: How to Manage Your Employees When They're All Carrying Guns"
- The Art of Charm, "Ep. 561: Dan Ariely | Payoff"
- The Art of Charm, "Ep. 539: Shawn Blanchard | From Miscreant to Mentor"
- The Art of Charm, "Ep. 417: Olaniyi Sobomehin | I'm Not You"
- The Art of Charm, "Ep. 399: Ramit Sethi | Cold Truths About Networking and Success"
- The Art of Charm, "Ep. 326: Alex Kouts | The Art of Negotiating"
- The Art of Charm, "Ep. 302: Arel Moodie | The Art of Likability"
- Tai Lopez' "Book of The Day" Show, "The Simple Steps to Finding Direction in Your Career and Life"
- Tai Lopez' "Book of the Day" Show, "How to Network — The Power of The 5 C's"
- Freakonomics Radio, "When Willpower Isn't Enough"
- Freakonomics Radio, "The Upside of Quitting"

Made in the USA
Columbia, SC
20 May 2018